Abingdon Worship Annual 2019

CONTEMPORARY &
TRADITIONAL
RESOURCES FOR
WORSHIP LEADERS

Abingdon Worship
Annual 2019

✢

Edited by
Mary J. Scifres
and B.J. Beu

Abingdon Press / Nashville

The Abingdon Worship Annual 2019

CONTEMPORARY AND TRADITIONAL RESOURCES
FOR WORSHIP LEADERS

Copyright © 2018 by Abingdon Press

This book is printed on acid-free paper.

ISBN 978-1-5018-5776-8

18 19 20 21 22 23 24 25 26 27—10 9 8 7 6 5 4 3 2 1

MANUFACTURED IN THE UNITED STATES OF AMERICA

Contents

May

June

July

August

September

October

November

December

Indexes

2019 Lectionary Calendar

Introduction

Planning and leading worship is a unique calling that challenges the best of us. It seems like only yesterday when worship planners were praised for coordinating scripture with liturgy, preaching, and hymns. And if the choir anthem actually fit the theme, worship was considered amazing. Now, worship leaders are faced with demands for diverse music and worship styles, and eye-catching on-screen presentations. Add in multimedia, visuals, texting, tweeting, and visitors "liking" your church on Facebook (during worship), and the pressures placed upon worship planners can become overwhelming.

To help you meet the demands of this awesome responsibility, we offer *The Abingdon Worship Annual 2019* as a resource and partner in your planning process. In this resource, we provide theme ideas and all the written and spoken elements of worship, following the Revised Common Lectionary. (Although the *Worship Annual* does not address the visual and emerging resources that many worship services require, Mary's *Worship Resource Subscription* provides all of these materials at **https://www.maryscifresministries.com/worship-resources**.) *The Abingdon Worship Annual 2019* offers words for worship that provide the framework for congregation to participate fully in the liturgical life of worship.

In *The Abingdon Worship Annual 2019*, you will find the words of many different authors, poets, pastors, laypersons, and theologians. Some authors have written for this resource before, others provide a fresh voice. Since the contributing authors represent a wide variety of denominational and theological backgrounds, their words will vary in style and content. Feel free to combine or adjust the words within these pages to fit the needs of your congregation and the style of your worship. (Notice the reprint permission for worship given on the copyright page of this book.)

For online access to the print materials, we include online access to each worship service at abingdonpress.com/downloads. (Simply click on the link to *The Abingdon Worship Annual 2019*, and when prompted, enter the password found on page 296) The web link allows you to import printed prayers and responsive readings directly into your bulletins for ease of use and printing.

Each entry provides suggestions that follow an order of service that may be adapted to address your specific worship practice and format. Feel free to reorder or pick and choose the various resources to fit the needs of your worship services and congregations. Each entry follows a thematic focus arising from one or more of the week's scriptures.

To fit the Basic Pattern of Christian Worship—reflecting a flow that leads from a time of gathering and praise, into a time of receiving and responding to the Word, and ending with a time of sending forth—each entry includes Contemporary Gathering Words, Call to Worship and Opening Prayer, Prayer of Confession and Words of Assurance, Response to the Word, Offertory Prayer, and Benedictions. Communion resources are offered in selected entries. Additional ideas are also provided throughout this resource.

Some readers find the Contemporary Gathering Words or Unison Prayers helpful as "Centering Words" that may be printed in a worship handout or projected on a screen. Use the words offered here in the way the best suits your congregation's spiritual needs, and please remember to give copyright and author credit!

Using the Worship Resources

Contemporary Gathering Words and **Calls to Worship** gather God's people together as they prepare to worship. Often called "Greetings" or "Gathering Words," these words may be read by one worship leader or responsively. Regardless of how they are printed in this resource, feel free to experiment in your services of worship. They may be read antiphonally (back and forth) between two readers or two groups within the congregation: women and men, choir and musicians, young people and old, etc.

Opening Prayers in this resource are varied in form, but typically invoke God's presence into worship. Whether formal, informal, general, or specific, these prayers serve to attune our hearts and minds to God. Although many may be adapted for use in other parts of the worship service, we have grouped them into the category "Opening Prayers."

Prayers of Confession and **Words of Assurance** lead the people of God to acknowledge our failing while assuring us of God's forgiveness and grace. Regardless of how they are printed, whether unison or responsively, Prayers of Confession and Words of Assurance may be spoken by a single leader or led by a small group. Some prayers may even be used as Opening or Closing Prayers.

Litanies and **Responsive Readings** offer additional avenues of congregational participation in our services of worship. Think creatively as you decide how to use these Responsive Readings in your service of worship: in unison, by a worship leader alone, or in a call and response format. Feel free to change the title of these liturgies to suit your worship setting.

Benedictions, sometimes called "Blessings" or "Words of Dismissal" send the congregation forth to continue the work of worship. Some of these Benedictions work best in call and response format, others work best when delivered as a blessing by a single worship leader. As always, use the format best suited to your congregation.

In response to requests from many of our readers, we have provided a number of **Communion** liturgies as well, each written specifically to relate to the thematic and scriptural focus of the day. Some follow the pattern of the Great Thanksgiving; others are Invitations to Communion or Communion Prayers of Consecration for the celebration of the Eucharist.

Although you will find *The Abingdon Worship Annual 2019* an invaluable tool for planning worship, it is but one piece of the puzzle for worship preparation. For additional music suggestions, you will want to consult *Prepare! An Ecumenical Music and Worship Planner* or *The United Methodist Music and Worship Planner*. These resources contain lengthy listings of lectionary-related hymns, praise songs, vocal solos, and choral anthems. As a final complement to your worship planning process, Mary also pens *Worship Plans and Ideas* as part of her worship subscription service, including video and film clip suggestions, screen visuals, popular song ideas, hands-on participation suggestions, along with series ideas, suggested sermon titles, and sermon starters for each Sunday. Explore Mary's *Worship Resource Subscription* at https://www.maryscifresministries.com/worship-resources.

As you begin your worship planning, read the scriptures for each day, then meditate on the **Theme Ideas** suggested in this resource. Review the many words for worship printed herein and listen for the words that speak to you. Trust God's guidance, and enjoy a wonderful year of worship and praise!

Mary J. Scifres and B. J. Beu, Editors
The Abingdon Worship Annual
beuscifres@gmail.com

January 1, 2019

Watch Night/New Year
Joanne Carlson Brown

Color
White

Scripture Readings
Ecclesiastes 3:1-13; Psalm 8; Revelation 21:1-6a; Matthew 25:31-46

Theme Ideas
This is a time of new beginnings—a time to reflect on the promises of newness and possibilities—God is making all things new. It is also a time to reflect on the fact that there is a time for everything under heaven. We are called to renew our covenant with God—the covenant to be the people God calls us to be—to be God's hands and feet in the world; and to bring the message that in God's realm, there is comfort, love, justice and a chance to begin anew.

Invitation and Gathering

Centering Words (Eccl 3)
There is a time and a season for every purpose under heaven.

Call to Worship (Ps 8)
Come, people of God. Come and worship our God.
How majestic is your name in all the earth.
Come, people of God. Come and worship the God who cares for us.
We give thanks to our loving and caring God.
Come, people of God. Come and worship the God who has crowned us with glory and honor.
We celebrate the God of glory and wonder.

—Or—

Call to Worship (Rev 21)
This is the day of new beginnings.
We give thanks for newness of life.
Today, God dwells with us.
We celebrate that we are God's beloved people.
Today, all things are made new.
Let us worship God, the alpha and omega.

Opening Prayer (Eccl 3)
O God of all seasons and purposes under heaven,
    we come in this season of new beginnings
        to pray for guidance
            in all the aspects of our lives.
Help us to remember that no matter what happens,
    you are always with us—
        in times of joy and sadness, life and death,
            silence and speech, dancing and mourning,
                war and peace.
May we always live in such a way
    that we reflect the glory to your name.
As we are mindful of the past,
    let us rejoice in the future.

We pray in the name of the God
of all of our days and ways. Amen.

Proclamation and Response

Prayer of Confession (Matt 25)
Ever present, ever loving God,
we come to this new year
mindful of the things we have done
and left undone in the past.
Forgive the times when we did not reach out in love
to the least of your sons and daughters.
Forgive us O God,
when we closed our eyes
to the sight of people
living in rags on the street;
when we stopped our ears
to cries of those who are lonely;
when we turned away from the sight
of swollen, malnourished bodies.
Help us to see you in everyone we meet.
Help us to be your hands, feet and voice in this world.
May we work for a world where no one is a stranger,
and where all will be welcomed into your glory.
Amen.

Words of Assurance (Matt 25)
Our God is a God of compassion and love,
ready to forgive all who truly repent
and desire to live a life of justice and love.
Know that the God who calls us
to be members of God's family,
will welcome you with open arms of grace
and forgiveness.

Passing the Peace
>   This is a season of peace—a season of hopeful expectation as we enter the coming year. Let us share signs of the promise of this season as we pass the peace of Christ. (B. J. Beu)

Response to the Word (Eccl 3)
>   For everything there is a season.
>   **And in each season of our lives, God is with us:**
>   in our laughter and in our tears,
>   **in our dancing and in our mourning,**
>   in our silence and in our speech,
>   **in our fighting and in our peacemaking.**
>   For everything there is a season.
>   **And God is with us.**

Thanksgiving and Communion

Offering Prayer (Isa 63, Ps 65, Heb 2, Matt 2)
>   Ever-loving God, we come to this new year
>   with hopes and dreams, fears and doubts.
>   As we step across the threshold of this new year,
>   may we have confidence in your abiding presence
>   in all the myriad aspects of our lives.
>   Open us to all the possibilities and promises
>   that a new year can bring.
>   In gratitude for your many blessings,
>   we bring our gifts before you now.
>   May our offerings be signs
>   of your new heaven and new earth—
>   signs that all people will soon live with you
>   in justice and peace. Amen.

Sending Forth

Benediction (Eccl 3)

Go forth, rejoicing that our God is with us
in all times and places,
and in all the seasons of our lives.

—Or—

Benediction (Rev 21)

Go forth into the new year, trusting in God's promises.
And may God, the alpha and the omega,
be with you always.

January 6, 2019

Epiphany of the Lord
Deborah Sokolove

Color

White

Scripture Readings

Isaiah 60:1-6; Psalm 72:1-7, 10-14; Ephesians 3:1-12; Matthew 2:1-12

Theme Ideas

God is not limited by time or space. The good news of Christ is available to everyone. Like Paul who came to know Christ in a vision, or the Magi who followed a star to the birthplace of Jesus, we are called to witness to the love and goodness of God in every time and place, by caring for all who are in need.

Invitation and Gathering

Centering Words (Isa 60)

Arise, shine, for your light has come. The glory of God's goodness and grace has risen upon you that you may show God's love in all that you do. Arise, shine, for your light has come.

Call to Worship (Isa 60, Eph 3, Matt 2)
Arise, shine, for your light has come,
and the glory of God's goodness and grace
has risen upon you.
**We come like the Magi, following the star
of the Christ child.**
Arise, shine, for your moment has come,
and the glory of God's love and mercy
flows through you into the world.
**We come like Paul, to share the good news
that Christ lives among us.**
Arise, shine, for you are called to be God's people,
and to bring good news and great joy
to a world that yearns for wholeness and peace.
Let us worship the God who calls us.

Opening Prayer (Isa 60, Eph 3, Matt 2)
Bright, shining Maker of visions and dreams,
the good news of your love
lights up the world with radiant glory.
We see you in rain and snow,
in sunrise and sunset,
in the smiles and hugs and celebrations
that greet the new year.
Like the Magi who followed a star
to welcome the newborn Christ,
help us follow the star of your love
and bring gifts of wholeness and peace
to a world that is broken and in pain;
Share with us the boundless riches of your grace,
that we might be bearers of your goodness,
in the name of Jesus, who is the Christ,
now and in the days to come. **Amen.**

7

Proclamation and Response

Prayer of Confession (Isa 60, Ps 72, Matt 2)
Holy Protector of all who are in need,
the words you place within our hearts
shine like a guiding star,
calling us to show the world
your goodness and your grace.
Heal us with your steadfast love
when we close our minds
and shutter our hearts,
refusing to let your brightness
shine through us.
You call us to protect widows and orphans,
and to care for all who have no helper.
Restore us in your mercy
when we put our own comfort
before the needs of others,
and when we are unwilling
to stop the oppression and violence
done in our name.
You promised to reveal your glory through us,
and proclaimed that we will shine like the sun
when the world is plunged into shadows.
Renew us in the power of your Spirit
when we refuse to follow the star
you have placed before us.

Words of Assurance (Isa 60, Matt 2)
The Holy One fills us with the brightness of Christ,
and makes us shine like a star in the deepest night.
In the name of Christ you are forgiven.
In the name of Christ you are forgiven.
Glory to God. Amen.

Passing the Peace of Christ (Isa 60)
> Rejoicing in the brightness of God's blessings, let us share signs of peace.
> The peace of Christ be with you.
> **The peace of Christ be with you always.**

Response to the Word (Matt 2)
> Holy God of life and grace, we give you thanks
> > for the word you have placed in our hearts,
> > > that shines like a star to guide our way.
> **Help us to bring your bright to the world**
> > **and shine your love into in every place**
> > **of shadow and fear.**

Thanksgiving and Communion

Offering Prayer (Matt 2:1-12)
> Bright, shining Maker of visions and dreams,
> > accept the gifts we bring you this day,
> > > that they may shine like a star,
> > > > brightening all the world with your grace.
> Amen.

Great Thanksgiving
> Christ be with you.
> > **And also with you.**
> Lift up your hearts.
> > **We lift them up to God.**
> Let us give our thanks to the Holy One.
> > **It is right to give our thanks and praise.**

> It is a right, good and joyful thing,
> > always and everywhere to give thanks to you,

who set a star in the sky to guide the Magi
as they searched for the holy Child
and warned them to go home by another way.

And so, with your creatures on earth
and all the heavenly chorus,
we praise your name and join their unending hymn:
Holy, holy, holy Lord, God of power and might,
heaven and earth are full of your glory.
Hosanna in the highest. Blessed is the one
who comes in the name of the Lord.
Hosanna in the highest.

Holy are you, and holy is your child, Jesus Christ,
who showed himself to Paul,
so that through his testimony
all the world might hear the good news
of your goodness and grace.
On the night in which he gave himself up,
Jesus took bread, broke it and said:
"Take, eat, all of you.
This is my body, broken for you.
Whenever you eat it,
do so in remembrance of me."
After supper, he took the cup, saying:
"Drink this, all of you.
This is the cup of the new covenant,
poured out for the healing of the world.
Whenever you drink it,
do so in remembrance of me."

And so, in remembrance of your mighty acts
in Jesus Christ, we proclaim the mystery of faith.
Christ has died.
Christ is risen.
Christ will come again.

Pour out your Holy Spirit on us
and on these gifts of bread and cup.
Make them be for us the body and blood of Christ,
that we may offer light and hope
to a world that is broken and in pain.
To you, who are the only true light,
we give our thanks and praise.
Amen.

Sending Forth

Benediction (Isa 60, Matt 2)
Like the Magi who followed the star,
let the light of God shine through you
and in you and all around you.
In the name of the Source of all light,
the shining Spirit and the one, true Light;
go in peace to love and serve the world.
Amen.

January 13, 2019

Baptism of the Lord

Mary Scifres

Color

White

Scripture Readings

Isaiah 43:1-7; Psalm 29; Acts 8:14-17; Luke 3:15-17, 21-22

Theme Ideas

Baptism of the Lord Sunday celebrates not only God's beloved child Jesus, but all who are named and claimed as God's honored and beloved children. Isaiah reminds the Israelites of their rightful identification as God's honored and beloved children. These words echo down through the ages to all who accept God's naming through our own baptismal rituals and remembrances. This glorious God, whose voice is strong enough to break the cedars of Lebanon, gives voice to love at Jesus' baptism and claims us as gloriously created beloved children, honored sisters and brothers of Christ.

Invitation and Gathering

Centering Words (Isa 43, Luke 3)
Beloved children of God, come to the river of life. Hear
the loving voice of God: "You are my beloved children."

Call to Worship (Isa 43, Luke 3)
Come to the river of life.
Listen for the words of love.
Come to the waters of grace.
Receive the gift of acceptance.
Come to the river of love,
for all are welcome here.

Opening Prayer (Isa 43, Luke 3)
Glorious God, we rejoice in your presence
on this holy day.
Reveal your presence to us in word and sacrament,
in fellowship and worship.
Speak words of life,
that we may sense your Spirit
breathing new life into us
each and every day.
Speak your words of love,
that we may rest in the knowledge
that we are your beloved children.
In your holy name, we pray. Amen.

Proclamation and Response

Prayer of Confession (Isa 43, Luke 3)
Beloved One, when we forget
that we are your beloved children,
draw us ever closer to you.

When we fail to hear your voice of love,
      whisper your words of reassurance.
When we don't reflect the divine image within us,
      forgive us.
Wash over us with your mercy and grace,
      and bathe us in your abundant love,
            that we may remember who we are
            and whose we are.
In your holy name, we pray. Amen.

Words of Assurance (Isa 43)
Don't fear—God is with us.
Christ has redeemed us
      and claims us as God's own—
            children named and honored
            with compassion and love.

Passing the Peace of Christ (Isa 43, Luke 3)
As beloved children, as one family of God, let us share signs of belonging and love with one another as we pass the peace of Christ.

Introduction to the Word (Isa 43)
From the east, God has called us here.
From the west, God has gathered us together.
From the north, we have been reclaimed.
From the south, we have been renewed.
Gather now as one community of beloved children,
      as we listen for the word of God.

Response to the Word (Isa 43, Luke 3)
Who are you?
      A beloved child of God.
Who am I?

A beloved child of God.
Who are we?
Beloved children of God!

Thanksgiving and Communion

Invitation to the Offering (Isa 43)
As God has gathered us together, let us join together to
share our gifts with God's people, that all may know
they are all beloved children of God.

Offering Prayer (Luke 3)
Beloved God, bless these gifts
    with your loving presence.
Bless our very lives with your Holy Spirit,
    that we may be signs of your mercy and grace
        in the world.
In your loving Spirit, we pray. Amen.

Sending Forth

Benediction (Isa 43, Luke 3)
Go to love one another,
    for you are beloved.
Go to honor one another,
    for you are honored.
Go to share life with one another,
    for you have been given life.
Go with the power of God,
    whose Spirit is always with us,
    always guiding us.

January 20, 2019

Second Sunday after the Epiphany
Rebecca J. Kruger Gaudino

Color

Green

Scripture Readings

Isaiah 62:1-5; Psalm 36:5-10; 1 Corinthians 12:1-11; John 2:1-11

Theme Ideas

Today's readings focus on the overflowing love of God. The psalmist praises God's steadfast love as a "river of…delights" and a "fountain of life" (36:8-9 NRSV). John tells the story of Jesus turning jars brimming with water into the finest wine to please the wedding feast's guests. Paul speaks of the Spirit giving Jesus' followers a full range of gifts that enliven the faith community to God's wisdom and knowledge (the Greek word for *activates* in verses 4 and 11 is the root of the word *energy*). These texts convey God's abundant love—a love that bring us joy, comfort, purpose, and enlightenment.

Invitation and Gathering

(Consider setting the stage for worship with a small fountain. Put a microphone beside it if it is quiet. If there is opening music, ask for it to be spare, so the sound of the fountain can be heard threading through the music. Consider having the sound of the fountain as background for different parts of worship. Have a table set with pitchers and jars of water. Or project photos of fountains, rivers, overflowing pitchers and jars on a screen.)

Centering Words (Ps 36)

Fountain of Life, well up in me.

Call to Worship (Ps 36)

God, your steadfast, never-giving-up love is so huge
that it fills the heavens.
Your faithfulness is so vast
that it rises to the clouds.
Under your loving wings,
we find comfort and refuge.
In your house of love,
we sit around the table feasting.
Your life and love are like a fountain in our lives.
You are the love-filled Light
that allows us to see and understand.
O God, your faithful love is precious to us!

Opening Prayer (Ps 36, 1 Cor 12)

Take a moment to speak with somebody near you, if you wish, about how you have experienced or observed God's love in your or someone else's life this week.
(Allow 1–3 minutes.)
Join me in our opening prayer.

We stand in your house of love
and remember the many ways
you have blessed us with faithful love.
Your love is like a fountain in our lives,
welling up in ordinary, everyday ways,
and in unexpected, extraordinary ways.
We stand in your presence with thankful hearts,
grateful that your love fills the cosmos
and gives us life. Amen.

Proclamation and Response

Prayer of Confession (Ps 36)
From the very start, you have loved us, God.
But there are times and circumstances in our lives
when we're not always so sure where your love is.
When things become really tough
and sometimes wonder where you are,
losing our sense of hope
that your love will always be there.
No matter where we are today—
feeling hopeful or facing despair—
let your fountain of life flow anew in our lives:
bringing us and our deserts to life,
watering our lives in their thirsty places.
We pray in your powerful name. Amen.

Words of Assurance (Ps 36)
God's steadfast love fills the cosmos.
It beckons us to take refuge,
and comforts us in tough times,
so draw near.
You are in the right place.

This is the house of love.
You are accepted no matter what.
God is the Fountain of Life—
    the fountain that waters our thirsty lives!

Passing the Peace of Christ (Ps 36, 1 Cor 12)
Let us pass the peace of Christ to all who have entered this house of love!

Introduction to the Word (Ps 36)
The psalmist tells us that in God we find the fountain of life. Let us listen for life-giving words.

Response to the Word (Ps 36, 1 Cor 12, John 2)
God, let your steadfast love flow in our lives.
Jesus Christ, fill our lives to the brim with your glory.
Holy Spirit, energize us with your gifts.

Thanksgiving and Communion

Invitation to the Offering (Ps 36, 1 Cor 12)
We belong together in this house through the love of God that draws us together. We also know that God's love extends to the cosmos, so let us share our love with others through our gifts and our service of every kind.

Offering Prayer (Ps 36)
Because of your generosity to us, God of love,
    we have courage to be generous.
Bless our gifts.
May they bring acts of generous love
    to make it clear that your love extends
        beyond the doors of this house.
The entire cosmos is your house of love. Amen.

Sending Forth

Benediction (Ps 36, 1 Cor 12)
We stand together in this house of love,
each of us having received amazing love
and gifts of grace from God.
We leave this house, bearing God's love to others,
that everyone might experience
the joy, hope, courage and gifts of God.
Go in love to serve God.

January 27, 2019

Third Sunday after the Epiphany
Deborah Sokolove

Color

Green

Scripture Readings

Nehemiah 8:1-3, 5-6, 8-10; Psalm 19; 1 Corinthians 12:12-31a; Luke 4:14-21

Theme Ideas

We rejoice in the evidence of God's word acting in the natural world, in scripture, and in our lives. We rejoice in the good news that Jesus brings to all who are oppressed, in need, or broken in body or spirit. We rejoice that we are members of the body of Christ, each of us using our gifts for the healing of the world.

Invitation and Gathering

Centering Words (Ps 19, 1 Cor 12, Luke 4)

As members of Christ's body, we are called to witness to the goodness of God, the goodness of creation, and the good news that Jesus proclaimed.

Call to Worship (Ps 19, 1 Cor 12, Luke 4)

Holy, loving Creator of all,
the heavens declare your goodness each day
and night proclaims your love.
You call us to witness to your power and grace.
You give us mouths to sing your praises,
hands and feet to do your will.
You call us to proclaim the good news
of your reign.
We yearn to become your people, the body of Christ,
living for the sake of the world.
Let us worship the God who calls us.

Opening Prayer (Ps 19, 1 Cor 12, Luke 4)

Surprising, sustaining Giver of grace,
you make us part of your holy body,
awakening us with glimpses of your glory.
You allow us to see shadows of your astonishing beauty
in the deep, bright blue of the winter sky.
Your frosty breath leaves sheets of shimmering ice
on windshields and doorsteps.
You make our words write trails of steam
in the crisp morning air.
You invite us into your very breath—
as the Holy Spirit breaths us into awareness
of your loving presence.
In our prayers, in our songs, and in our silence,
teach us how to be your holy body,
to bring good news to world that yearns for you.
Amen.

Proclamation and Response

Prayer of Confession (Ps 19, Luke 4)
> Holy One, we often forget to rejoice
> > in the gift of each new day.
> We close our ears to the voices
> > of rivers and streams—
> > > voices that sing your praises
> > > > day and night.
> We close our eyes to the need of our neighbors,
> > and refuse to see their suffering and pain.
> We close our hearts to your proclamations
> > of hope and freedom—
> > > proclamations of good news
> > > > and release for all who live
> > > > > in oppression and fear.
> Forgive us when we keep your good gifts
> > closed tightly in our own fists.

Words of Assurance (1 Cor 12, Luke 4)
> Hear the Good News:
> > God forgives us and loves us,
> even when we forget that we are meant
> > to be good news for the world.
> In the name of Christ, you are forgiven.
> > **In the name of Christ, you are forgiven.**
> > **Glory to God. Amen.**

Passing the Peace of Christ (Ps 19)
> Rejoicing in God's many gifts, let us greet one another
> with signs of peace.
> The peace of Christ be with you.
> > **The peace of Christ be with you always.**

Response to the Word (1 Cor 12, Luke 4)
> Holy God of life and grace, we give you thanks
> for making us part of your body.
> > **Help us be the hands and feet,**
> > **and the eyes and ears,**
> > > **that bring your good news**
> > > **to all who are in need. Amen.**

Thanksgiving and Communion

Offering Prayer (Luke 4)
> Persistent, embracing giver of life,
> > use these gifts and offerings to bring good news
> > to all who suffer or are oppressed.
> **Amen.**

Great Thanksgiving
> Christ be with you.
> > **And also with you.**
> Lift up your hearts.
> > **We lift them up to God**
> Let us give our thanks to the Holy One.
> > **It is right to give our thanks and praise.**

> It is a right, good and joyful thing,
> > always and everywhere to give thanks to you,
> > who gave your word to the people
> > in the time of Ezra.
> You continue to speak to us now
> > through the teachings of Jesus,
> > and through every breath of our bodies,
> > every beat of our hearts.

We thank you for millions of stars;
    for oceans and rivers and uncountable raindrops;
    for stark branches scratching out wordless songs
    on a sullen sky;
    for the gifts of the earth and the work
    of human hands.

And so, with your creatures on earth
    and all the heavenly chorus,
    we praise your name and join their unending hymn:
    Holy, holy, holy One, God of power and might,
        heaven and earth are full of your glory.
    Hosanna in the highest. Blessed is the one
        who comes in your holy Name.
    Hosanna in the highest.

Holy are you and holy is your Son, Jesus Christ,
    who proclaimed the year of your favor,
    promising good news for the poor
    release for the captives,
    restoration of sight for those who cannot see,
    and that all who are oppressed will go free.

On the night in which he gave himself up,
    Jesus took bread, broke it, saying:
    "Take, eat, all of you.
    This is my body, broken for you.
    Whenever you eat it, do so in remembrance of me."
After supper, he took the cup, saying:
    "This is the cup of the new covenant,
    poured out for the healing of the world.
    Whenever you drink it, do so
    in remembrance of me."

And so, in remembrance of your mighty acts
in Jesus Christ, we proclaim the mystery of faith.
Christ has died.
Christ is risen.
Christ will come again.

Pour out your Holy Spirit on us,
and on these gifts of bread and cup.
Make them be for us the body and blood of Christ,
and make us all members of the body of Christ,
nourished for the healing of the world.
Amen.

Sending Forth

Benediction (Ps 19, 1 Cor 12, Luke 4)
Rejoicing in the good gifts of our Creator,
and filled with the joy of the Holy Spirit,
let us go out to love and serve the world
as the body of Christ.
Go to be good news to all who are in need.
Amen.

February 3, 2019

Fourth Sunday after the Epiphany

B. J. Beu

Color

Green

Scripture Readings

Jeremiah 1:4-10; Psalm 71:1-6; 1 Corinthians 13:1-13; Luke 4:21-30

Theme Ideas

God is with us and knows us before we are even born. The psalmist proclaims that this God, who took each of us from our mother's womb, is our rock and our refuge. Jeremiah is called to trust this God to tell him what to say and how to speak—for God puts words of prophecy in the mouths of God's servants. Jesus knew only too well the effect those words can have on communities, as his hometown almost threw him off a cliff when they heard him speak. And Paul warns that, while God knows us and gives us words to speak, we see only in part. What we share with the world is only part of a much larger truth—a truth that we will never fully understand until we see God face-to-face. It is more important to love well than to speak with the tongues of angels or to unfold all mysteries. This is sobering advice to individuals and religious communities that would rather instruct others in the word of God than share with others the love of God.

Invitation and Gathering

Centering Words (Jer 1, Ps 71, 1 Cor 13)

God has been with us and knew us before we were even born. The one who calls us to love has been loving us longer than we have drawn breath. Sink into the arms of Love this day and trust the hand that holds you.

Call to Worship (Ps 71)

Praise God from whom all blessings flow.
We are here to offer God our worship and praise.
Before God formed you in your mother's womb,
God knew you.
Before we drew our first breath,
God consecrated us in holy love.
Let us worship the one who knows and loves us.
Let us worship the one who is our rock
and our fortress in times of trouble.
Praise God from whom all blessings flow.
We are here to offer God our worship and praise.

Opening Prayer (Jer 1, 1 Cor 13)

Wrap us in the arms of your love, Holy One,
as we gather in worship this day.
Teach us to be patient and kind in our actions,
and humble of heart in all of our ways.

Help us see and know ourselves
as well as you see and know us,
that our words may be true
and our love may be pure.
Build us into a community that bears all things,
believes all things, and hopes all things
in the name of Love, which never ends. Amen.

Proclamation and Response

Prayer of Confession or Prayer of Yearning (Jer 1, 1 Cor 13)
God of truth and love,
when we yearn for certainty in an uncertain world,
remind us that we know only in part;
when we long for others to see things our way,
remind us that we see in a mirror dimly;
when we seek to impose our ways upon others,
remind us that we have failings of our own.
Harken us to your voice once more,
and reveal to us the truths that you alone can see.
In your holy name,
we seek your guidance now. Amen.

Words of Assurance (Jer 1, Ps 71, 1 Cor 13)
The one who formed us in our mothers' wombs
looks upon us with love and seeks our highest good.
Rejoice in the good news that we are fully known,
and that we are loved with a love
that heals all wounds and breaks down all barriers
that lie between us.

Passing the Peace of Christ (1 Cor 13)
Now faith, hope, and love abide as signs of God's care
for us. Let us share these signs with one another as we
pass the peace of Christ.

Response to the Word (1 Cor 13)
Source of love and light,
at the beginning of a new week,
we need your blessing to get us through.
As we meditate on the hearing of your word,
remind us once more what is truly important:
Love is patient.
Love is kind.
Love is not envious.
Love is not boastful.
Love is not arrogant or rude.
Love does not insist on its own way.
Love does not rejoice in the wrong
but rejoices in the right.
Love bears all things.
Love believes all things
Love hopes all things.
Love endures all things.
Love never ends.
Bless us with this love, O God,
today and all days.
Amen.

Thanksgiving and Communion

Invitation to the Offering (1 Cor 13)
With faith leading the way, with hope lighting our path,
and with love leading us home; let us open our hearts as
we share with the world the wondrous gift of love.

Offering Prayer (Jer 1, Ps 71, 1 Cor 13)
> Source of every good gift,
>> you have watched over us
>>> all the days of our lives—
>>>> guiding our ways,
>>>> protecting us from harm,
>>>> and showering us with your blessings.
> Receive these offerings from our grateful hearts,
>> and bless the world with our heartfelt thanks,
>>> that all might know your amazing gift of love.
> Amen.

Sending Forth

Benediction (Jer 1, 1 Cor 13)
> God sends us forth with words of love on our lips.
> Christ sends us forth with acts of love in our deeds.
> The Spirit sends us forth with the spirit of love
>> sustaining our very lives.
> Go in the power of God's love
>> and be ambassadors of Christ's love and peace.

February 10, 2019

Fifth Sunday after the Epiphany
Mary Scifres
[Copyright © Mary Scifres. Used by permission.]

Color

Green

Scripture Readings

Isaiah 6:1-8 (9-13); Psalm 138; 1 Corinthians 15:1-11; Luke 5:1-11

Theme Ideas

God's call pervades today's scripture readings. Isaiah exclaims, "Here am I; send me!" In the Gospel of Luke, James and John leave everything behind to follow Jesus. Paul recognizes that his call to proclaim God's message is a gift of grace that allows him to do what he was created to do. The psalmist sings of this truth with these words: "The Lord will fulfill [God's] purpose for me" (Psalm 138:8a NRSV). Throughout this season after Epiphany, scripture reminds us of the myriad ways that God calls each and every one of us. It also reminds us of the challenge we face, even when we gladly answer, and quickly follow, that call.

Invitation and Gathering

Contemporary Gathering Words (Isa 6, 1 Cor 15, Luke 5)
> From fishing fleets and busy harbors,
>> God gathers simple sailors.
> Through persecution and injustice,
>> God calls brave prophets.
> When we least expect it,
>> Christ gathers us in,
>> and calls to follow him.
> Let us gather and answer Christ's call.

Call to Worship (Isa 6, Luke 5)
> Called by God, we have come to worship.
> **Called by Christ, we have come to follow.**
> Called by the Spirit, we have come to rejoice.
> **Called together, we will listen and pray.**

Opening Prayer (Isa 6, Luke 5)
> Holy God, we gather to sing your praise
>> and hear your word.
> Speak to us now,
>> that we may be wise enough
>>> to perceive your call.
> Strengthen us now,
>> that we may be brave enough
>>> to answer when you call.
> Guide us now,
>> that we may follow
>>> where you would have us go.

Proclamation and Response

Prayer of Confession (Luke 5)
>Master, we have worked all day and night,
>>for many months and years.
>We yearn for a heavy catch,
>>a full church, an abundant feast.
>Forgive us God,
>>when we are too tired
>>>to cast our nets one time;
>>when we are too stubborn
>>>to do things a little differently.
>Have mercy on us,
>>when we are too afraid
>>>to dive into deep waters
>>>>and take a risk.
>Grant us grace,
>>that we may proclaim your word,
>>>work for your kingdom,
>>>>and trust your promises. Amen.

Words of Assurance (Luke 5)
>Do not be afraid! Christ has called.
>Christ has redeemed us.
>Christ will save us all.

Introduction to the Word(1 Cor 15, Luke 5)
>Hold firmly to the message of Christ. Delve into the lessons of God. Hear God's word, and heed Christ's call, and you will live.

Response to the Word (Luke 5)
>When all seems pointless, and it's easy to give up:
>**We will drop our nets in the deep.**

When the harvest is scarce and the needs are great:
We will drop our nets in the deep.
When Christ calls for disciples and speaks to your heart:
We will drop our nets in the deep.

Thanksgiving and Communion

Invitation to the Offering (Isa 6)
Whom should God send? Who will go for God's people? Here we are, God is counting on us. Let us share our gifts and our offerings in answer to God's call.

Offering Prayer (Ps 138, Luke 5)
Increase the strength of these gifts,
and the strength of our ministries, O God.
Expand the nets of our love,
that we may reach deeply
and share abundantly.
In Christ's name, we pray.

Invitation to Communion (Luke 5)
Come into the deep water of God's love. Cast your nets into the miraculous waters of Christ's grace. Drink of the living water, eat of the bread of life, for this is the table of abundant love.

Great Thanksgiving (Luke 5)
The Lord be with you.
And also with you.
Lift up your hearts.
We lift them up to the Lord.
Let us give thanks to the Lord our God.
It is right to give our thanks and praise.

It is right, and a good and joyful thing,
    always and everywhere to give thanks to you,
    almighty God, creator of heaven and earth.
In ancient days, you created us in your image,
    and called us to be your people.
Even when we turned away and ignored your voice,
    you pursued us and called us:
    through the proclamation of your law,
    the words of your prophets,
    and the wisdom of your poets and storytellers.
In the fullness of time, you sent your Son, Jesus Christ
    to call us yet again:
    on the shores of Galilee,
    in crowded markets, and on dusty roads,
    inviting us to risk everything,
    and to place our trust in you.

And so, with your people on earth,
    and all the company of heaven,
    we praise your name
    and join their unending hymn, saying:
    Holy, holy, holy Lord, God of power and might,
        heaven and earth are full of your glory.
    Hosanna in the highest. Blessed is the one
        who comes in the name of the Lord.
    Hosanna in the highest.

Holy are you and blessed in your Son, Christ Jesus,
    who called to his disciples,
    even as he shared a final meal with them,
    calling one and all to remember and reflect
    when we eat of the bread and partake of the cup.

"Take, eat; this is my body, given for you.
Do this in remembrance of me."
"Drink from this, all of you.
This is my life, poured out for you and for many
for the forgiveness of sins.
Do this, as often as you drink it,
in remembrance of me."

And so, in remembrance of these
your mighty acts of love and grace,
we offer ourselves in praise and thanksgiving
as we proclaim the mystery of faith.
Christ has died.
Christ is risen.
Christ will come again.

Communion Prayer (Luke 5)
Pour out your Holy Spirit
on all of us gathered here,
that we may answer your call
and be your people.
Pour out your Holy Spirit
on these gifts of bread and wine,
that they may nourish and strengthen us
to go into deep waters
when you call us to take a risk.
By your Spirit, make us one with Christ,
one with each other,
and one in ministry to all the world,
until Christ comes in final victory
and we feast at your heavenly banquet.
Through Jesus Christ,
with the Holy Spirit in your holy Church,

all honor and glory is yours, almighty God,
    both now and forevermore. Amen.

Giving the Bread and Cup

(The bread and wine are given to the people, with these or other words of blessing.)
The bread of life, strengthening you,
    to answer Christ's call.
The living water, blessing you,
    to live in faith and grace.

Sending Forth

Benediction (Luke 5)

Listen for God's word.
Answer Christ's call.
Go into the deep and love courageously.
Rejoice in the harvest of grace!

February 17, 2019

Sixth Sunday after the Epiphany

B. J. Beu

Color

Green

Scripture Readings

Jeremiah 17:5-10; Psalm 1; 1 Corinthians 15:12-20; Luke 6:17-26

Theme Ideas

The blessings and woes of Jesus' sermon on the plain capture the tone and theme of today's scriptures. Jeremiah and the psalmist contrast the blessing of the righteous, who are like trees planted by streams of water, with the curse of the wicked, who are like shrubs that wither and in the desert. Likewise, Jesus contrasts the blessings in store for those who are poor and who suffer now with the woes in store for those who are rich and comfortable. These scriptures describe both the blessings of God's kingdom and the consequences of putting earthly rewards above heavenly blessings. They highlight the blessings gained from trusting God, and the loss incurred when we turn away from God. The epistle argues for belief in the resurrection and does not fit these themes.

Invitation and Gathering

Centering Words (Jer 17)
Those who place their trust in God are like trees planted by streams of water, bearing fruit in due season and with leaves that are ever green.

Call to Worship (Jer 17)
Blessed are those who trust God,
whose trust is the Lord.
> **They are like trees planted by water,**
> **sending out roots by the stream.**
They have no fear of summer's heat,
nor do they wither in the sun.
> **In the year of drought they are not anxious,**
> **for their lives bear the fruit of righteousness.**
Come to the waters of life
all you who trust in the Lord.
We have come to worship
and to send forth our roots
into streams of God's living water!

Opening Prayer (Luke 6)
God of blessings and woes,
> bless us this day with lives filled with love,
> > caring, generosity, and deep, abiding hope.
We pray that your kingdom will dwell among all people,
> and that we may be instruments of your love
> > and your grace.

Open our hearts with the joy
    of healing a world filled with brokenness
        and pain.
In the name of the one
    who taught us the ways of light and love,
        be in our worship and in our very lives. Amen.

Proclamation and Response

Prayer of Confession or Prayer of Yearning (Jer 17, Ps 1)
Gentle guide, loving guardian,
    heal our foolish ways.
We long to forsake the advice of the wicked
    and the slow seduction of sinful paths,
        but our speech and actions often belie us.
We yearn to be like trees planted beside living waters,
    bearing the fruit of righteousness in due season,
        but the seat of scoffers calls to us
            and the temptation to return evil for evil
            withers our souls
                like shrubs in the desert.
Our hearts seek the ways of your Spirit
    and the waters of life,
        but our footsteps lead us into arid, desert sands.
This is not your hope and plan for us.
Forgive us.
Turn us again to the healing you so freely offer,
    and mend the brokenness in our lives
        and in our world. Amen.

Words of Assurance (Luke 6)
God looks at us in our brokenness,
    and offers blessings to all who turn to the Lord.
With the assurance of God's faithful love,
    choose this day to be people of blessing.

Passing the Peace of Christ (Jer 17, Ps 1)

Those who place their faith in the Lord are blessed. Let us share this blessing with those around us as we pass the peace of Christ.

Invitation to the Word (Ps 1)

Let us delight on the law of God,
and meditate on God's teachings, day and night.

Response to the Word (Ps 1)

Those who delight in the law of God,
and who meditate on God's teachings, day and night,
are like trees planted by streams of water.
**Hearing God's word, we send our roots
into streams of living waters.**
Those who heed the words of God
bear the fruit of righteousness.
Living God's word, our leaves are ever green.

Thanksgiving and Communion

Invitation to the Offering (Jer 17, Ps 1, Luke 6)

God has blessed us with lives that bear much fruit. Let us share the blessings we have received from God with those in need as we collect today's offering.

Offering Prayer (Jer 17, Ps 1, Luke 6)

Source of every blessing,
you have planted us beside living waters
and nourished our souls with your ways of life.
In gratitude and thanks
for the fruit we have born in due season,
we return these gifts to you.

Bless them with your manifold grace,
and multiply them in your mercy,
that they may go forth to heal a world
trapped in loneliness and isolation.
In the name of the one who leads us into life,
we pray. Amen.

Invitation to Communion (Luke 6)
Blessed are you who hunger,
for you will be filled at Christ's table.
We come to Christ's table
with a hunger for justice
and a thirst for righteousness.
Blessed are you who weep,
for you will be comforted at Christ's table.
We come to Christ's table
with hearts seeking joy and laughter.
Blessed are you who suffer for your faith,
for you will find solace at Christ's table.
We come to Christ's table
with spirits yearning for healing and strength.
Come to the table, for all are welcome here.

Sending Forth

Benediction (Jer 17)
Go from this place as those who are blessed.
We will live in God's love.
Go from this place as trees planted beside living waters.
We will drink of Christ's mercy.
Go from this place to bear the fruit of righteousness.
We will share the Spirit's strength
with everyone we meet.

February 24, 2019

<u>Seventh Sunday after the Epiphany</u>

B. J. Beu

[Copyright © B. J. Beu. Used by permission.]

Color

Green

Scripture Readings

Genesis 45:3-11, 15; Psalm 37:1-11, 39-40; 1 Corinthians 15:35-38, 42-50; Luke 6:27-38

Theme Ideas

Today's scriptures address questions relevant to our time: "How are we supposed to treat others?" and "Does God's love extends to all?" In Genesis, God sends Joseph into Egypt to save the world from famine. The psalmist warns us not to grow angry because the wicked are prospering, for God will soon set everything right and give sinners their just desserts. As we saw last week, Jesus' sermon on the plain begins with blessings for the poor and suffering, and woes to the rich and comfortable. But today's continuation of that sermon moves beyond crime and punishment. The Golden Rule teaches us to do unto others as we would have them do unto us—regardless of whether they are friend or foe, saint or sinner. Indeed, God is kind to even ungrateful sinners. How we choose to focus these scriptures determines how we answer the questions asked above. But Jesus makes clear that the crime and punishment paradigm has been replaced with the Golden Rule—no matter how annoyed and angry people make us.

Invitation and Gathering

Centering Words (Luke 6)
Love is an all or nothing proposition. Only by loving your enemies as well as your friends do you live as children of the Most High.

Call to Worship (Luke 6)
Come and learn the ways of life.
We have come to follow Jesus.
Love your enemies,
and do good to those who hate you.
We have come to follow Jesus.
Bless those who curse you,
and pray for those who persecute you.
We have come to follow Jesus.
Do unto others as you would have them do unto you.
We have come to follow Jesus.
Come and learn the ways of life.

Opening Prayer (Luke 6)
Inexhaustible source of love and life,
be with us in our time of worship
as we seek the love it takes
to walk in the ways of your Son.

Help us love our enemies
and bless those who wrong us,
for we cannot do so alone.
Teach us the joy of treating others
with all the same respect and goodness
with which we hope to be treated.
May our every word and deed make known
that we are your beloved children
and vessels of your love. Amen.

Proclamation and Response

Prayer of Confession or Prayer of Yearning (Ps 37, Luke 6)
Teacher of hard truths,
it is difficult to let go of our anger
toward those who prosper through deceit
and unscrupulous ways;
it is not easy to make ourselves believe
that the meek will inherit the earth,
when they are being crushed
by the unjust systems
stacked against them.
We long to see the vindication of the righteous
and the prosperity of those who work selflessly
to bring your realm here on earth.
We yearn for the day
when all people will treat one another
as they wish to be treated.
Help us live into that day, Holy One,
even when it is difficult,
that your love might shine like the sun
through our lives and our ministries. Amen.

Words of Assurance (Luke 6)

> When we treat others as we would have them treat us,
> Jesus calls us beloved children of the Most High.
> If God is kind to the ungrateful and the wicked,
> how much more will God be kind to those
> who love the Lord and seek to live the Golden Rule?
> Rest in this assurance and be at peace.

Passing the Peace of Christ (Luke 6)

> Let us be known as children of the Most High by sharing our love with all as we pass the peace of Christ.

Invitation to the Word (Ps 1)

> Let us delight in the law of the Lord,
> and meditate on God's teachings, day and night.

Response to the Word (Luke 6)

> Let us be known as children of the Most High.
> **We will love our enemies,**
> **and do good to those who hate us.**
> Let us be known as disciples of Christ.
> **We will bless those who curse us,**
> **and pray for those who wrong us.**
> Let us be known as heirs of the Spirit.
> **We will be merciful,**
> **even as our God is merciful.**

Thanksgiving and Communion

Invitation to the Offering (Luke 6:38 NRSV)

> Jesus said, "Give, and it will be given to you. A good measure...running over, will be put into your lap; for the measure you give will be the measure you get back."

Offering Prayer (Gen 45, Luke 6)
>Source of every blessing,
>>as you sent Joseph into Egypt
>>>to save the world from famine,
>>>>you sent Jesus into our lives
>>>>>to save us from selfishness and greed.
>For teaching us to treat others
>>as we would have them treat us,
>>>we give you our thanks and praise.
>Bless these gifts,
>>that we have received from your bounty,
>>>and send them forth to those in need.
>>>>whether they be friend or foe.
>For all are your beloved children
>>and our sisters and brothers. Amen.

Sending Forth

Benediction (Luke 6)
>Go with God's blessings.
>>**As followers of Jesus,**
>>**we will love our enemies**
>>**and do good to those who hate us.**
>Go with God's blessings.
>>**As followers of Jesus,**
>>**we will bless those who curse us**
>>**and pray for those who persecute us.**
>Go with God's blessings.
>>**As followers of Jesus,**
>>**we will do unto others**
>>**as we would have them do unto us.**
>Go with God's blessings.

March 3, 2019

Transfiguration Sunday

B. J. Beu

Color

White

Scripture Readings

Exodus 34:29-35; Psalm 99; 2 Corinthians 3:12–4:2; Luke
9:28-36, (37-43a)

Theme Ideas

The mystery and wonder shrouding God's holiness is
central in today's scripture readings. The psalmist ex-
tols the glory and majesty of God—the one who sits en-
throned upon the cherubim. And just as Moses' face was
radiant from being in God's presence, so too Jesus was
transfigured upon the mountaintop with Moses and Elijah. The essence of glory is mystery, and the essence of
mystery is wonder.

Invitation and Gathering

Centering Words (Exod 34, Ps 99, Luke 9)
The mystery of God calls us here. With the eyes of your heart enlightened, behold the glory of God and bask in wonder.

Call to Worship (Exod 34, Luke 9)
Climb with Moses up the mountain of God.
God's glory shines like the sun.
Climb with Jesus up the mountain of God.
Christ's glory shines like the sun.
Climb with the faithful up the mountain of God.
The Spirit's glory shines like the sun.
Climb the mountain of God.
We have come to see and to worship.

Opening Prayer (Exod 34, Luke 9)
Source of awe and mystery,
as your presence caused Moses' face
to shine with your glory,
may your presence in our time of worship
cause our lives to shine with your glory.
Reveal the glory of Christ to us this day,
as you revealed it to Peter, James and John
on that mountaintop long ago.
Transform our worship with the light of discovery,
that our souls might shine the light of Christ
into a world in need of your love. Amen.

Proclamation and Response

Prayer of Confession or Prayer of Yearning (Exod 34)
God of majesty and might,
we imagine the face of Moses

shining with the radiance of your glory;
we pretend that we would not look away in fear
or feel relieved when he shielded our eyes
from the effects of your power;
we imagine being commended for our courage
in the face of your splendor—
but we know better.
We long to be invited like Peter, James, and John
to witness Christ's glory,
but we secretly suspect that we too
would be weighed down with sleep,
or feel the need to speak
when we should be listening.
Test our hearts, O God.
Call us to climb your mountain,
that we might face our fears
and prove ourselves worthy
of your holy calling. Amen.

Words of Assurance (Luke 9)

Jesus was transfigured on the mountaintop
to show us the power and the glory of God.
In the light of Christ's glory,
know that we are made whole
through the love and grace of God.

Passing the Peace of Christ

See the light of Christ shining in those around you, as
you greet one another with words of Christ's peace and
signs of God's love.

Response to the Word (Exod 34, Ps 99, Luke 9)

The majesty of God is too great for you to bear.
We will not shy away.

The mystery of God is too deep for you to fathom.
We will not turn away.
The glory of Christ is too bright to behold.
We will not look away.
Thanks be to God.

Thanksgiving and Communion

Offering Prayer
Lord of Light, when we become complacent
and fail to see the wonder of your presence,
you bless us with your radiance and your love.
Illumine these gifts,
that the world may see your light
shining in our gifts and our offerings.
Illumine our very lives,
that our souls may shine like Christ
as he was transfigured upon the mountaintop.
Amen.

Sending Forth

Benediction (Exod 34, Luke 9)
Go forth to climb the mountain of God.
We will walk in the light and truth of God.
Go forth and listen to the voice that calls from heaven.
We will heed the call to follow Jesus.
Go forth to shine the light of Christ in the world.
We will live as lamps shining in the darkness.
Go with God.

March 6, 2019

Ash Wednesday
Karen Clark Ristine

Color

Black or None

Scripture Readings

Joel 2:1-2, 12-17; Psalm 51:1-17; 2 Corinthians 5:20b–6:10; Matthew 6:1-6, 16-21

Theme Ideas

We turn our hearts more fully toward the Divine in the season of Lent. Ash Wednesday sets our focus. We examine our lives and work to eliminate habits that distract us from the holy. We ask our Creator to create our hearts anew. We turn more fully toward Christ so that our hearts are aligned to our treasure.

Invitation and Gathering

Centering Words (Matt 6)
Turn your eyes upon Jesus,
> look full in his wonderful face.
> —Helen H. Lemmel

Call to Worship (Joel 2, Ps 51)

Return to me with all your heart, says the Lord.
We open our hearts to soulful examination.
Return to the Lord who is gracious and merciful.
We open our hearts to God's steadfast love.
With your hearts open to the Lord,
what do you seek?
Create in me a clean heart, O God,
and put a new and right spirit within me.

Opening Prayer (Joel 2, Ps 51)

God of graciousness and steadfast love,
welcome us anew this day
into an inward, spiritual journey
of self-examination.
We turn our hearts to you
and seek renewed faith and conviction
to follow the Jesus Way.
As our own hearts fill with your love,
create in us a renewed spirit.
We treasure your presence in our lives
and on our Lenten journey. Amen.

Proclamation and Response

Prayer of Confession (Ps 51)

O God, we have turned from you
in our hearts, minds and actions.
We feel the distance we create
when we look away.
Whether our turning was deliberate or gradual,
conscious or almost unawares,
we return to you now with contrite hearts.

We open our lives before you
 and seek your gracious forgiveness.
We confess our need to return to you,
 to turn toward you as we journey in Lent
 toward Easter and the hope of resurrection.
Amen.

Words of Assurance (Ps 51)
 Through grace and forgiveness,
 the Lord restores the joy of our salvation
 and sustains in us a willing spirit.
 In the name of Jesus Christ, you are forgiven.
 In the name of Jesus Christ, you are forgiven.

Response to the Word (Matt 6)
 With our heavenly treasure stored within our very souls,
 we receive these holy scriptures
 and write them as promises
 that pray themselves in our hearts.

Thanksgiving and Communion

Offering Prayer (Matt 6)
 Loving Creator,
 receive the gifts of our earthly resources
 and accept the gifts of our love.
 May these earthly treasures
 lead others to follow your path of care
 for all humanity.
 And may our heavenly treasures
 inspire us to be your incarnation
 in the world. Amen.

Sending Forth

Benediction (2 Cor 5, Ps 51)

As servants of God, commend yourselves in every way
as you depart.
Open your hearts to God your Creator.
Set your hearts upon the love of Christ,
and follow the Holy Spirit with all your heart.
Amen.

March 10, 2019

First Sunday in Lent
Hans Holznagel

Color

Purple

Scripture Readings

Deuteronomy 26:1-11; Psalm 91:1-2, 9-16; Romans 10:8b-13; Luke 4:1-13

Theme Ideas

Lest we be tempted by superficial slogans and simple solutions, Lent invites us to a deeper spirituality, a longer memory of faith, and a wider, more complex witness of scripture and tradition. It invites us, like the ancient Israelites and Jesus in the desert, to recite and to deliberately *not* forget.

Invitation and Gathering

Centering Words (Rom 10, Deut 30)

God's word is not too hard, nor is it far away. Just listen: it is very near to you today. Find it on your lips and in your heart.

Call to Worship (Ps 91, Deut 26)
> Refuge Almighty, Fortress Most High,
> > **Deliverer, Dwelling Place, and Protector,**
> be a tent on our wilderness journeys.
> > **Send your angels as our guides,**
> > **that we may find you, find ourselves,**
> > **and remember who we are.**

Opening Prayer (Deut 26, Rom 10, Luke 4)
> Guide us today, O God,
> > into a season of examination.
> Show us our ancestors' ways:
> > journeying, even wandering, boldly;
> > remembering deliberately who they were
> > > and who we are.
> Guide us inward to the Word felt in our hearts,
> > and outward to the Word heard on the lips of others.
> Grant us a season of depth and courage, we pray. Amen.

Proclamation and Response

Prayer of Confession (Rom 10, Luke 4)
> Our confession, O God, is that we believe.
> We believe in the power and presence
> > of your goodness made flesh.
> In the face of big evils and little falsehoods,
> > may your Word make its way
> > > from our hearts to our lips.
> May we confess you,
> > as Jesus did in the wilderness.
> Fill us with your Holy Spirit, we pray.

Words of Assurance (Rom 10)
> The apostle Paul reminds us that God is generous
> > when people call out in faith.
> In the name of Jesus,
> > who is God's Word made flesh and raised to life,
> > let us embrace God's abundant life.

Response to the Word (Deut 26, Luke 4)
> Into whatever journey lies before us,
> > lead on, Holy Spirit; lead on.

Thanksgiving and Communion

Invitation to the Offering (Deut 26)
> With grateful hearts, let us share a portion of the bounty
> God has given us. We do so as an act of faith, and in sup-
> port of God's work in this congregation and the world.

Offering Prayer (Deut 26)
> God of signs and wonders,
> > from the first fruit of the ground,
> > > we offer you our gifts.
> Cultivate good thing in us, we pray,
> > for the sake of the world you love. Amen.

Sending Forth

Benediction (Ps 91)
> Embrace the journey.
> Fear not its depths.
> Expect angels.
> Find refuge in the shadow of God.
> Go in peace. Amen.

March 17, 2019

Second Sunday in Lent

B. J. Beu

Color

Purple

Scripture Readings

Genesis 15:1-12, 17-18; Psalm 27; Philippians 3:17–4:1; Luke 13:31-35

Theme Ideas

Stark contrasts weave these texts together: darkness and light, death and salvation, shame and glory, betrayal and fidelity. But in all things, we are called to wait for the Lord, who is our deliverance and salvation. In terrifying darkness, God enters into a covenant with Abram and promises that Abraham's yearning for a son will be fulfilled. At the same time, the psalmist calls us to be strong and take heart, for God is our light and our salvation. Adversaries may rise against us in war, but God saves the faithful, turning fear into shouts of joy. The epistle warns that enemies of Christ revel in shame, while true disciples shine in God's glory. And Jesus brushes off warnings about Herod's plan to kill him, because nothing will deter him from doing the works of God: healing the sick, preaching the good news, casting out demons. Today's readings provide rich imagery depicting the need to wait for the Lord and the choices we face in our journey of faith.

Invitation and Gathering

Centering Words (Ps 27)

Wait for the Lord. Be strong and take heart, for God is our light and our salvation.

Call to Worship (Ps 27)

Wait for the Lord. Be strong; take heart.
We will see the goodness of God
in the land of the living.
The Lord is our light and our salvation.
Whom shall we fear?
Though adversaries plot against us,
God protects us from harm.
Sing to the Lord with songs of joy.
Make melody to the Lord, our God.
Come, let us worship.

Opening Prayer (Ps 27, Luke 13)

God of embracing love,
gather us under the wings of your love,
even as Jesus longed to gather Jerusalem
into the arms of his love.
Send your Holy Spirit into our worship this day,
that we may be strengthen for the time ahead,
as we seek to walk faithfully with Christ

all the way to the cross.
Be our light and our salvation,
that we may live in your presence
and walk in your ways
all the days of our lives. Amen.

Proclamation and Response

Prayer of Confession or Prayer of Yearning (Gen 15, Ps 27, Phil 3)

Mysterious One, in the darkness of night,
you met Abraham's deepest fears.
We long to meet you
in the secret place of our dreams.
Come to us in our darkest nights,
and overcome our fear and dread
with your hope and promise of new life.
Help us be strong and take heart,
for you are our light and our salvation.
Your power draws us like a moth to the flame.
Teach us your ways, O God,
that we may be your beloved children—
children of life and promise. Amen.

Words of Assurance (Luke 13)

Christ's desire is to gather us together,
as a mother hen gathers her brood under her wing.
Be strong; take heart,
for God's love and mercy pursue us,
even in the darkest night.
Thanks be to God!

Passing the Peace of Christ (Ps 27)
>Believing that we will see the goodness of God in our fellowship today, let us share signs of this goodness as we pass the peace of Christ.

Response to the Word (Gen 15, Ps 27)
>God's mercy meets us
>>in the darkness of our deepest fears,
>>>healing our weaknesses
>>>>and shining the light of love
>>>>>into the shadows of our lives.
>God is the light of our salvation;
>>whom shall we fear?
>Wait for the Lord.
>Be strong; take heart,
>>and we will see God's goodness
>>>in the land of the living.

Thanksgiving and Communion

Offering Prayer (Gen 15, Ps 27)
>God of light,
>>your blessings are as numerous as the stars;
>>your mercy is as deep as the sea.
>When we had no future,
>>you gifted us with a heritage that endures.
>For gathering us into your embrace
>>like a mother hen gathers her chicks,
>>>and for your many blessings,
>>>>we offer you our tithes and offerings.
>May these gifts be a source of blessing for others,
>>that all might know the promise of your goodness
>>>in the mean places of the world.

Sending Forth

Benediction (Isa 62, Ps 36)

Go forth in hope:
The Lord is our light and our salvation.
In God, we are not afraid.
Go forth in courage:
The Lord is our shelter from the storm.
In God, we dwell secure.
Go forth in peace:
The Lord embraces us in the arms of love.
In God, we find our true home.

March 24, 2019

Third Sunday in Lent
Mary Sue Brookshire

Color

Purple

Scripture Readings

Isaiah 55:1-9; Psalm 63:1-8; 1 Corinthians 10:1-13; Luke 13:1-9

Theme Ideas

Not all food nourishes us; not all drinks quench our thirst. Isaiah reminds the people not to waste their resources on the things that do not satisfy. Together with the words from the psalmist, today's Hebrew Bible passages affirm that seeking God is the path to fulfillment. The epistle tells us that the same spiritual food and drink that strengthened our ancestors in faith is our food and drink today. We are filled when we listen for the voice of God and when we cling to God with our whole being.

Invitation and Gathering

Centering Words (Isa 55, Ps 63)

God knows your thirst. God senses your hunger. Come,
eat and drink. A rich feast awaits you.

Call to Worship (Isa 55, Ps 63)

Welcome to the fabulous feast that God has prepared!
We come hungry, thirsty, and searching for God.
God is near, full of power and glory.
We are here to be fed by God's word.
Lift up your hands in praise!
We will sing with joy on our lips.
Bless God, who upholds us with God's strength.
We will bless God as long as we live!

Opening Prayer (Isa 55, Ps 63)

Faithful God, our parched spirits thirst for you.
Gathered here in your sanctuary,
may we witness again
your power and glory.
Feed our hungry souls
with the food that truly satisfies.
Quench our dry mouths
and fill them with your praise.
Be known to us here,
as we seek you with our whole being. Amen.

Proclamation and Response

Prayer of Confession (Isa 55)

Nurturing One, you invite us to feast on your word
and to be filled with your love.

Your banquet is always before us,
  freely offered for us to enjoy,
    yet we choose to spend our resources
      on things that do not satisfy.
Forgive us when we consume the very things
  that do not feed us.
Help us abandon our careless ways
  and self-seeking schemes,
    that we might return to you,
      our provider and sustainer.

Words of Assurance (Ps 63, 1 Cor 10)
  God is faithful and will not allow us to be tempted
  beyond our abilities.
    Even in our brokenness,
    God provides a path to wholeness.
  When we confess our shortcomings,
    God has mercy on us
    and is generous with forgiveness.
  Through Christ Jesus, we are forgiven.
    Thanks be to God.

Introduction to the Word (Isa 55)
  Listen carefully to the Word of God. Listen, and you will
  live.

Response to the Word (Ps 63, 1 Cor 10)
  Jesus, Living Water,
    you are the spiritual rock from which we drink.
  Continue to quench our thirsty souls,
    as we ponder and meditate on your word.

Thanksgiving and Communion

Invitation to the Offering (Ps 63)
Generous God, your faithful love
is a constant blessing.
As we have been blessed,
so may we now be a blessing to others.

Offering Prayer (Isa 55, Ps 63)
As we enjoy the rich feast you have provided,
we know that there are those who want
for food and drink.
Multiply the offerings we share today,
that they may bless those in need.
May the spiritual nourishment we receive today
strengthen us for continued service
in your name. Amen.

Sending Forth

Benediction (Isa 55, Ps 63)
Our search for God continues.
Our hunger and thirst will return.
Seek God in all places.
Seek God with your whole being.
We will call on God
and know that God is near.

March 31, 2019

Fourth Sunday in Lent
Karin Ellis

Color

Purple

Scripture Readings

Joshua 5:9-12; Psalm 32; 2 Corinthians 5:16-21; Luke 15:1-3, 11b-32

Theme Ideas

On this Fourth Sunday in Lent, these scriptures remind us of the renewing power of God's forgiveness. Joshua tells us that the Israelites have wandered in the desert for a while, but God is gracious. The people find a land where they are able to restore their relationship with God, settle in long enough to plant crops, and gather in the harvest. The psalmist utters words that can heal hearts. When we come before God and confess our sins, God's steadfast love and forgiveness lead us to new life and new relationships. The epistle vividly portrays becoming a new creation in Christ. And finally, we have the well-known story of the Prodigal Son from the Gospel of Luke. A son who wandered away and squandered his entire inheritance finds forgiveness from his father. May the father's open arms remind us that God embraces us with loving affection and forgiveness, and sets us on a new path where righteousness, hope, and peace fill our days!

Invitation and Gathering

Centering Words (Luke 15)
You are welcome here. No matter where you have been, no matter what you have done, you are welcomed in love and grace. May you find rest and renewal; may you find hope and peace. This is what God offers to us all!

Call to Worship (Ps 32, Luke 15)
To those who eagerly came to worship God,
>	**you are welcome here.**

To those who grumbled about coming,
>	**you are welcome here.**

To those who are not sure why they are here,
>	**you are welcome here.**

In the name the One who loves and forgives us,
you are welcome in this place.
>	**Thanks be to God!**

Opening Prayer (2 Cor 5)
Almighty, creating God,
>	you have called us to this place.

You breathe life into us each day.
You welcome us just as we are,
>	with all of our hopes and fears,
>>		all of our faults and talents.

As we worship, may we rest in your Spirit,
>	and may we remember that you alone
>>		renew our lives.

Help us shake off all that weighs down,
    that we may be free to hold fast to you,
        the One who fills our lives with unmerited grace
        and abounding love.
In the name of Christ, your Son, we pray. Amen.

Proclamation and Response

Prayer of Confession (Ps 32)
Loving God, we come before you
    knowing that you love us completely.
With this knowledge,
    we confess to you our wrongdoings.
Forgive us, Holy One,
    when we stray from your ways;
    when we hurt one another;
    when we ignore the needs of others;
    when we resist your guidance in our lives.
Gracious God, accept our prayers
    and hold us in your love,
        that we may be the people you call us to be.
In the name of Christ we pray. Amen.

Words of Assurance (Ps 32)
The Lord forgives our sins and washes away our guilt.
Brothers and sisters, "be glad in the Lord and rejoice,"
for our hearts have been made right with God!

Passing the Peace of Christ (2 Cor 5)
In Christ, everything is made new; we become a new
creation. In this Spirit, I invite you to greet one another with the peace of Christ and see Christ's presence in
each other.

Prayer of Preparation (Luke 15)

Almighty God, you have welcomed us here today.
Open our ears to your word.
Open our hearts to the movement of your Spirit.
Open our hands to receive your grace
    and to serve your people. Amen.

Response to the Word (2 Cor 5)

May the words we have heard
    become actions of love and forgiveness in our lives,
    that all may come to know new life in Christ.
Amen.

Thanksgiving and Communion

Invitation to the Offering (Josh 5)

Our God provides for our bodies, our souls, and our minds. In thanksgiving and praise, let us bring our gifts to God.

Offering Prayer (2 Cor 5)

Holy One, you provide for us
    in all ways and at all times.
We offer these gifts to you,
    asking for your blessing upon them,
        that they bring comfort and healing
            to your children around the globe.
We offer our lives to you,
    asking for your blessing upon us,
        that we might be faithful to you,
            and to one another.
In your precious and holy name, we pray. Amen.

Sending Forth

Benediction (2 Cor 5)
Go in peace to be ambassadors for Christ.
Go in forgiveness to be instruments
of the love of Christ,
and the comfort of the Holy Spirit.

April 7, 2019

Fifth Sunday in Lent

B. J. Beu

Color

Purple

Scripture Readings

Isaiah 43:16-21; Psalm 126; Philippians 3:4b-14; John 12:1-8

Theme Ideas

Our Hebrew scriptures remind us to remember the power of God's mighty deeds in the past as we face trials in the present. For the one who has saved Israel will surely do so again. Our New Testament scriptures tell us that all other considerations must be set aside when considering our relationship with Christ. Paul explains that all the gains he had before are nothing compared to what he has gained in Christ. And Jesus tells his disciples that whatever value that costly nard might bring if sold was nothing compared to the value of the gift of anointing him for his burial. We should draw strength and confidence from the past, but our present is inextricably linked to our relationship with God in Christ.

Invitation and Gathering

Centering Words (Ps 126)

Knowing Jesus changes everything. Meeting love incarnate changes everything. Are we ready to be changed?

Call to Worship (Isa 43, John 12)

The one who parted the waters to save Israel
will set our feet on dry land.
We will walk forward in faith.
The one who restored the fortunes of Zion
will fill our mouths with laughter
We will dream of life renewed.
The one who raised Jesus from the dead
will do a new thing in our lives.
We will rest in the peace of Christ.
Come, let us worship the God of our salvation.

Opening Prayer (Isa 43, Ps 126, Phil 3)

Lead us, Lord, into the mystery of your presence.
As we gather in this time of worship,
free us from the fears that bind us,
that our hearts may be filled with joy
and our tongues may sing your praises.
Teach us the glory of knowing your son,
and help us know the joy
that comes from loving freely.
Guide us in your ways and renew our hope,
that we may perceive signs of your Spirit
springing forth from your abundant love.
With joy-filled trust, we pray. Amen.

Proclamation and Response

Prayer of Confession or Prayer of Yearning (Ps 126, John 12)
> Merciful One, signs of your love and compassion
> > surround us every waking minute of each day.
> As we come before you with our quiet hopes
> > and our secret fears,
> > > we long to be like those who dream.
> We yearn for hearts that are filled with laughter
> > and for tongues that are lifted in shouts of joy.
> But too often, our quiet hopes remain unspoken,
> > and our secret fears remain hidden away.
> You alone are our hope and our salvation, O God.
> Anoint us with your mercy and compassion,
> > that we might have the courage
> > > to claim the life that springs forth all around us.
> Transform us into people who meet doubt with hope,
> > and despair with determination.
> In your loving mercy, we pray. Amen.

Words of Assurance (Isa 43, Ps 126, Phil 3)
> Hold fast to God's saving acts of old.
> For the one who parted the waters for Israel
> > is the one who raised Jesus from the dead.
> This is the one who will raise us also
> > from all that holds and binds us.

Passing the Peace of Christ (John 12)
> As Mary anointed Jesus with sweet smelling perfume,
> let us anoint one another with the sweetness of God's
> love as we share the peace of Christ.

Invitation to the Word (Isa 43)
> Listen for God's word of hope with new ears and fresh

faith. The words we read are not a testimony to God's acts in ancient history, they are an assurance of what God is doing now in our very midst. Listen for God's word of promise...for God is still speaking.

Response to the Word (Isa 43, John 12)

You have anointed us with your word, O God,
>   as surely as Jesus was anointed with perfume
>   by one who loved him.
May the sweetness of your ways bless us this day
>   and all the days of our lives.
May the presence of your Spirit bless us,
>   as you fulfill your promise
>   to do a new thing in our lives
>   and in our world. Amen.

Thanksgiving and Communion

Offering Prayer (Isa 43, Ps 126)

For your many blessings, O God,
>   we give you thanks and praise.
Your goodness springs forth
>   and blesses the dry ground
>   with live-giving waters.
You have restored our fortunes and given us a joy
>   that no force on earth can shake.
Bless these gifts from our good fortune
>   that we return to you now.
Through these gifts, and through our very lives,
>   bring forth new hope, new beginnings,
>   and new life for your people everywhere.
Amen.

Sending Forth

Benediction (Isa 43, Ps 126)

Go with hope, for God makes a way in the wilderness
and rivers in the desert.
We go forth to follow the ways of our God.
Go forth with faith, for Christ travels this road with us
and never leaves our side.
We go forth to walk in the ways of Christ.
Go forth in peace, for the Spirit is nearer to us
than our very breath.
We go forth to live in the ways of the Spirit.
Go with God's blessings.

April 14, 2019

Palm/Passion Sunday

Mary Scifres

Color

Purple

Palm Sunday Readings

Psalm 118:1-2, 19-29; Luke 19:28-40

Passion Sunday Readings

Isaiah 50:4-9a; Psalm 31:9-16; Philippians 2:5-11; Luke 22:14–23:56

Theme Ideas

This is a day of fortune reversal. Jesus' triumphal entry into Jerusalem to a cheering crowd soon gives way to a tragic trial and a jeering mob. The blessings of a sacred last meal ends with a series of tragic prophecies. A quiet night of prayer is overcome by a violent crowd, ending in an arrest. And so begins our Holy Week, a week of sorrow, but a week when we also prepare for another reversal of fortune on Easter Sunday.

Invitation and Gathering

Centering Words (Luke 19, Ps 118, Luke 23)
> Give thanks. Sing Hosanna. Bless the one who comes in
> the name of the Lord. But prepare yourself, for hosannas
> will quickly give way to cries for crucifixion.

Call to Worship (Luke 19, Ps 118)
> With songs of thanksgiving,
> > **we sing praise to God.**
> With shouts of Hosanna,
> > **we welcome the presence of Christ.**
> With prayers of blessing,
> > **we call out to the Spirit of God.**
> Come, Holy Spirit, come.

Opening Prayer (Luke 19, Luke 22)
> Blessed One, bless our worship this day.
> Bless us through the power of your holy name,
> > that we may be faithful disciples
> > > and attentive listeners.
> Strengthen us with your Holy Spirit,
> > that we may be ever wakeful, ever alert—
> > > as we worship,
> > > as we live,
> > > and as we follow where you lead.
> In your blessed name, we pray. Amen.

Proclamation and Response

Prayer of Confession (Ps 31, Luke 22, Luke 23)
> Have mercy on us, O God.
> Where depression lingers,

grant us hope.
Where fear threatens,
     grant us comfort.
Where strength fails,
     give us courage.
Where faithfulness wanes,
     grant us endurance.
Where sin invades,
     grant us forgiveness.
Shine upon us with your love and grace, O God.
In your blessed name, we pray. Amen.

Words of Assurance (Ps 118, Isa 50)
Look! The Lord will help you,
     for God's faithful love lasts forever.

Introduction to the Word (Phil 2)
May we listen with the mind of Christ.
May we listen with openness to being changed.
May we listen for the word of God.

Response to the Word (Luke 22, Luke 23)
Holy God, our future is in your hands.
Our Holy Week is in your hands.
Guide us on this journey,
     that we may be ever faithful,
     ever hopeful, and ever loving.
Broaden our perspective,
     that we may look for signs of life,
     even when death is all around.
Hosanna. Alleluia. Amen.

Thanksgiving and Communion

Invitation to the Offering (Ps 118)

This is the Lord's gate. This is God's house. This is God's world. All that we have and all that we are comes from God and belongs to God. May we share of these gifts generously, so that others may know God's presence in the world.

Offering Prayer (Ps 118, Phil 2)

With these gifts, we give you thanks, O God.
We bless your generous, humble spirit,
    and ask that you bless these gifts
        with this same generous, humble spirit,
            so that all who receive these gifts
                may also receive your love,
                    through Christ, our Lord. Amen.

Sending Forth

Benediction (Luke 23, Holy Week)

As darkness descends,
    may we ever look for the light.
As Holy Week begins,
    may we ever look for the resurrection.
Go in quiet contemplation.
Go in quiet hope.
Go in the love of God.

April 18, 2019

Holy Thursday

Mary Scifres

Color

Purple

Scripture Readings

Exodus 12:1-4, (5-10), 11-14; Psalm 116:1-4, 12-19; 1 Corinthians 11:23-26; John 13:1-17, 31b-35

Theme Ideas

This is a night of remembrance, but also a festival night. Just as the Israelites remembered the horrors of slavery in Egypt, they celebrated the release and freedom from bondage. Just as we remember the last supper and a precious time of humble footwashing, we celebrate the gift of Holy Communion and the sacred act of serving one another. This is a night of remembrance, but also a festival night.

Invitation and Gathering

Centering Words (1 Cor 11, John 13)
Friends, let us be servants of one another.
Let us break bread and share in this gift of love.

Call to Worship

God's love has called us here.
We come in the shelter of love.
Christ's service guides our steps.
We come in the service of God.
The Spirit's presence welcomes us all.
We come in the promise of blessing and renewal.

Opening Prayer (1 Cor 11, Luke 13)

Loving Christ, on this night of remembrance,
we remember your loving gift of life,
and we celebrate your presence amongst us.
Send your Holy Spirit upon us,
that we may sense your presence
and bathe in your grace.
Send your Holy Spirit on the sacred gifts
of bread, wine, water, and towel,
that they may become for us
your living presence,
full of mercy and grace.
In your loving name, we pray. Amen.

Proclamation and Response

Prayer of Confession or Prayer of Yearning (Ps 116, 1 Cor 11, John 13)

We love you, Lord.
But even in our love,
we cry out in need.
We cry out for strength in times of trial.
We long for hope in times of despair.
We yearn for mercy in the midst of our sin.
Strengthen us, O God,
and renew our hope.

Grant your mercy.
Feed us with the bread of forgiveness
    and the water of life,
        that we may courageously face our lives
            and gladly accept your grace.
In your loving name, we pray. Amen.

Words of Assurance (Ps 116, John 13)

Christ hears our cries with compassion,
    wipes away our tears with grace,
    and forgives our sins with mercy.
Rest assured that all is well. Amen.

Passing the Peace of Christ (John 13)

We have but one instruction this night: To love one another. Let us share signs of this love as we pass the peace of Christ.

Introduction to the Word(1 Cor 11)

May we remember.
May we give thanks.
May we prepare ourselves
    to receive this gift from God,
    for God's word is a sacred gift.

Response to the Word (John 13)

This new commandment to love
sounds like an old familiar friend.
This opportunity to serve
seems like a familiar Christian path.
As we remember the familiar call
to love and serve one another,
may we infuse the old with new commitment.
We will love and serve ever more passionately.

**We will rejoice in these ancient lessons,
and strive to live them more fully each day.**

Introduction to Footwashing (John 13)
May we remember.
May we give thanks.
May we prepare ourselves
    to serve and be served.
May we receive this gift from God with thanksgiving,
    for in serving one another,
    we are share the gift of God's love.
This is truly a sacred gift.

Thanksgiving and Communion

Offering Prayer (John 13)
Loving God, bless these gifts with love.
Send them forth to serve the world,
    even as you send us forth to one another.
Send them into the world with love,
    even as you send us into the world with love.
Loving God, bless us with love,
    that we may be love for the world.
In the name of love, we pray. Amen.

Sending Forth

Benediction (John 13)
As we have been served,
    we go now to serve.
As we have been loved,
    we go now to love.
Go in peace.

April 19, 2019

Good Friday, A Service of Tenebrae
B. J. Beu
[Copyright © B. J. Beu. Used by permission.]

Color

Black or none

Scripture Readings

Isaiah 52:13–53:12; Psalm 22; Hebrews 10:16-25; John 18:1–19:42

Tenebrae Readings

Although a traditional Service of Tenebrae contains sixteen readings taken from John 18:1–19:42, this service contains fourteen readings culled from all four Gospels. Just as no Christmas Eve service would be complete without the arrival of the magi, no passion account is complete without elements omitted from John's narrative. The readings conclude at Jesus' death, the climax of the passion narrative, and omit the two burial readings (John 19:31-37, and John 19:38-42), which may be included if desired.

Theme Ideas

Suffering, rejection, and loss focus our readings. Although the Isaiah passage begins with the exaltation of God's servant, it is a chilling reminder of how easily we turn on God's chosen ones. A Service of Tenebrae (or darkness) is an extended meditation of Christ's passion. Psalm 22, which Jesus quotes while hanging on the cross, conveys the sense of being abandoned by God when the forces of destruction hold sway. Peter's betrayal of his friend and teacher in the courtyard depicts how low we can sink, despite our love and convictions. *(Worship Note: If your congregation has a gold or brass cross on its Lord's Table, substitute a rough-hewn wooden cross with horseshoe nails at the place of Jesus' hands and feet.)*

Invitation and Gathering

Centering Words (John 1)

Where is the light that shines in the darkness? Where do we turn when all hope is lost?

Call to Worship

Were you there when they crucified my Lord?
We were the hollow echo
of hosannas once spoken in love.
Were you in the garden when the disciples fell asleep?
We were the betrayal in Judas's kiss.
Were you in the courtyard when the cock crowed?
We were the denial on Peter's lips.
Were you among the scoffers when Jesus was flogged?
We were the whip in the soldier's hand.
Were you in Pilate's chamber

when he washed his hands of Jesus' fate?
We were the hatred of the crowd,
and the indifference in Pilate's heart.
Were you with the powers of this world
when the soldiers dressed Jesus as a king?
We were the mockery in the crown of thorns.
Were you among the spectators at Golgotha?
We were the nails that pierced Jesus' hands
and feet.
Were you there when they crucified my Lord?
We were the silence when no bird sang.

Opening Song
"Were You There" (vv. 1–3)

Opening Prayer (Isa 52–53, Ps 22:1 NRSV)
Elusive One, O that our eyes were a fountain of tears
to weep for ourselves and our world.
Where do you go when all hope fades?
Where do you hide
when we cry out with the psalmist"
"My God, my God,
why have you forsaken me?"
In the midst of our pain and despair,
we strain to see you arriving in the nick of time.
Yet, in our disbelief and dismay,
we face the emptiness of your absence
and the ache of our despair.
Your ways are beyond us, Holy One,
shrouding us in mystery.
Be with us in our hour of greatest need,
most of all,
do not abandon us when we deny you.

Proclamation and Response

First Reading (Luke 22:39-53)
(The first candle is extinguished.)

Second Reading (John 18:12-14)
(The second candle is extinguished.)

Song
"Go to Dark Gethsemane" (vv. 1–2)

Third Reading (Luke 22:54b-62)
(The third candle is extinguished.)

Litany (John 18)
There is no warmth in the fire.
Our blood runs as cold as the night.
The one we love is in peril.
Our courage blows away like the wind.
Strangers recognize our fellowship with Jesus.
Our denial pierces the soul
like the cock's crow pierces the dawn.
There is no warmth in the fire.
Our tears flow as cold as the night.

Fourth Reading (John 18:19-23)
(The fourth candle is extinguished.)

Fifth Reading (Matt 27:1-2)
(The fifth candle is extinguished.)

Song
"When Jesus Wept" *(Taizé style)*

Sixth Reading (Matt 27:3-10)
(The sixth candle is extinguished.)

Litany (Matt 27)
Jesus stands condemned.
Wait! Stop this madness.
It is too late.
We repent of our sin.
You have been well paid.
We don't want your blood money.
It is yours all the same.
Please, stop this madness.
It is too late.

Seventh Reading (John 18:33-38)
(The seventh candle is extinguished.)

Song
"What Wondrous Love Is This"

Eighth Reading (Matt 27:15-24)
(The eighth candle is extinguished.)

Prayer of Confession or Prayer of Yearning (Matt 27)
Holy Mystery, our faith stands upon a knife's edge.
We long to stand up for what we believe,
  but it is easier to wash our hands of responsibility
    and to blame others for our inaction.
We yearn to take a principled and courageous stand,
  but it is easier to defer to the judgments of others
    and simply go along with the crowd.
We dream of following Jesus to the end,
  but it is easier to slip into the darkness
    and betray the spirit striving within us.
Forgive us, O God,
  and help us find our courage
    amidst the dying of the light.

Ninth Reading (Matt 27:26-31)
(The ninth candle is extinguished.)

Song
"O Sacred Head Now Wounded"

Tenth Reading (Matt 27:32-37; John 19:20b-21)
(The tenth candle is extinguished.)

Eleventh Reading (Luke 23:35, 39-43)
(The eleventh candle is extinguished.)

Song
"Jesus, Remember Me" *(Taizé style)*

Litany
Come to the cross and feel the weight of the world.
We bring the weight of our sins.
Come to the cross and feel the weight of the world.
**We bring the weight of our desertions
and our betrayals.**
Come to the cross and feel the weight of the world.
We bring the weight of our accusations
and our scorn.
Come to the cross and feel the weight of the world.
We bring the weight of our lives.

Twelfth Reading (Mark 15:33-34)
(The twelfth candle is extinguished.)

Thirteenth Reading (Mark 15:35-36)
(The thirteenth candle is extinguished.)

Fourteenth Reading (Matt 27:50-51)
> *(As the description of the earthquake is read, a loud noise is made by a symbol or other such instrument; then the fourteenth candle is extinguished.)*

Sending Forth

(Drape the cross with black cloth and extinguish the Christ candle. Have rubrics in the program for the people to depart in silence.)

April 21, 2019

Easter Sunday

Mary Scifres

[Copyright © Mary Scifres. Used by permission.]

Color

White

Scripture Readings

Acts 10:34-43; Psalm 118:1-2, 14-24; 1 Corinthians 15:19-26; John 20:1-18 (or Luke 24:1-12)

Theme Ideas (Acts 10, John 20, Luke 24)

The power of perspective drives the story of Easter Sunday. Are we looking for hope in the message of Jesus, the Christ? Are we prepared to discover life in the midst of death? Are we ready to receive faith in the midst of doubt? Even when we aren't sure what we're looking for, Christ comes. Christ lives. Christ is present. We are not alone, and both life and love win. This is the victory of the Easter story.

Invitation and Gathering

Centering Words (Acts 10, John 20, Luke 24)

Are you ready for hope? Are you ready for love? Are you ready for life? Surprise! Hope, love, and life win!

Hope, life, and love conquer all! Are you ready? Are you looking? Easter hope, life, and love are all around.

Call to Worship (John 20, Luke 24)
Look, life is here,
even when the tomb is empty.
Listen, love is calling,
even when death is all around.
Believe, for hope reigns victorious;
this is the gift of resurrection.
This is the miracle of Easter.
Hallelujah! Amen.

Opening Prayer (John 20, Luke 24)
Risen Christ, rise in our hearts with faith.
Raise our voices in praise,
and lift our eyes to the hills of hope.
Reveal to us your presence.
Raise us up to new life,
even as you were risen,
that we may proclaim to the world:
"Christ is risen!
Christ is risen indeed!"

Proclamation and Response

Prayer of Confession (John 20, Luke 24)
God of new life, where there is despair,
rise up in us with hope.
When we are buried in the tomb of our sin,
rise up in us with mercy and grace.
Bloom forth with grace in our lives,
that we might burst forth in promise,

and live with resurrection faith
each and every day.
With Easter joy, we pray. Amen.

Words of Assurance (1 Cor 15)

Give thanks and sing,
for God's faithful love conquers the grave,
covers us with grace, and raises us up
with new life and new beginnings.

Passing the Peace of Christ (John 20, Luke 24)

Look around for signs of life! Look around for signs of
joy! Let us share these signs with one another as we pass
the peace of Christ.

Prayer of Preparation (John 20, Luke 24)

Living Christ, prepare us once more
to hear your resurrection message.
Open our hearts to the joyous gift of life
shared with us this day.
And open our minds to your presence,
each and every day.

Response to the Word (John 20, Luke 24)

Look for life.
It's all around!
Live for love.
It's gift abounds!
Live with hope.
It's freely given!
Celebrate the risen Christ.
Christ is risen indeed!

Thanksgiving and Communion

Invitation to the Offering (John 20, Luke 24)
    Bring your hope. Bring your love. Bring new life, as you
    share your gifts with the Risen Christ.

Offering Prayer (John 20, Luke 24)
    Risen Christ, bring resurrection hope
        through these gifts we now bring!
    May they become signs of new life,
        and symbols of hope for a hurting world—
            a world yearning for the life-giving power
                of your saving love.

Sending Forth

Benediction (John 20, Luke 24)
    As we go forth with resurrection joy,
        may we bring Christ's living presence
        with our words, our actions, and our love.

April 28, 2019

Second Sunday of Easter
Joanne Carlson Brown

Color

White

Scripture Readings

Acts 5:27-32; Psalm 150; Revelation 1:4-8; John 20:19-31

Theme Ideas

To what do we witness? We have just celebrated the glorious resurrection, yet it seems more is needed for some folks to fully witness to the Risen Jesus. The texts for today are full of affirmations of the glory and power of God and of the Risen Jesus. In spite of threats of persecution and death, in spite of fear and doubts, people come to conviction to praise God and affirm Jesus as the Messiah. We are called to continue the witness that was given that Easter morning with praise and joy and affirmation: Jesus is Lord.

Invitation and Gathering

Centering Words

Out of despair comes hope. Out of fear comes affirmation. Out of threats comes conviction. Out of our hearts comes praise.

Call to Worship (Ps 150, John 20)

Even in the midst of our questions.

We will praise the Lord.

Even with fears of what might be.

**We will praise God for God's mighty deeds,
according to God's surpassing greatness.**

We come with faith that is growing in spite of this.

Praise God with song and dance.

Let us offer worship and praise to the living God,
the Risen Jesus, and the Holy Spirit.

**Let everything that breathes praise God.
Praise God!**

Opening Prayer (Acts 5, John 20)

Life-giving, Life-affirming God, we come this morning,
    remembering the joy of Easter
        while facing realities of this world.
Fill us with the hope of new life that resurrection brings.
Help us open our hearts to the never-ending,
    unconditional love of this Easter season.
Be with us now in our time of worship,
    and remain with us each and every day
        as we walk our paths of life in faith. Amen.

Proclamation and Response

Prayer of Confession (John 20)
> Ever patient and loving God,
>> the excitement and joy of Easter have faded,
>>> and our doubts and fears are creeping in again.
> We somehow need to see to believe.
> We long for the peace
>> that Jesus breathed on his disciples,
>>> but feel too vulnerable and afraid to ask.
> We long to affirm with Thomas:
>> "My Lord and my God,"
>>> but we sometimes lack the conviction.
> Forgive us our doubts, our fears, and our reluctance
>> to witness to you and to the Risen Jesus.
> We pray for the courage and conviction
>> of those first disciples—
>>> disciples who overcame their fear and doubt
>>>> to become mighty witnesses.
> Lord, we believe; help our unbelief. Amen.

Words of Assurance (Acts 5, Rev 1, John 20)
> The one who loves us and frees us
>> will not leave us in despair and doubt,
>> but will fill us with all joy and conviction.
> Let us praise and witness to the Holy One—
>> the one who says I am the Alpha and Omega,
>> the beginning and the end;
>> the one who is with us always.

Passing the Peace of Christ
> One of the most important things we will do this morn-
> ing is to share the love that we have been given uncon-

ditionally by God through Jesus. Let us share this love and joy and peace with one another.

Prayer of Preparation

Let us open the eyes and ears of our hearts, that we may hear the words of challenge and comfort that the Spirit brings us this morning.

Response to the Word (Acts 5, Ps 150, Rev 1, John 20)

For words of comfort in the midst of despair;
> for words of conviction in times of doubt;
> for words of witness in moments of indifference;
> for words of joy in times of sorrow,
> > we offer you thanks and praise, O God.

Thanksgiving and Communion

Invitation to the Offering (Acts 5, Ps 150, Rev 1, John 20)

We have been called to be witnesses to our faith. We have been called to do so with joy and praise. With hearts full of thanksgiving for all that we have received, let us commit ourselves and our resources to enable the church to be that fearless witness.

Offering Prayer (Acts 5, Ps 150, Rev 1, John 20)

In offering all that we are and all that we have to you,
> we witness to our faith
> > and pledge our commitment to you
> > > and to your world.

We do so with praise and thanksgiving,
> for your steadfast love and sustaining grace.

May the gifts we bring before you
> offer hope to a despairing and doubting world.

Amen.

Sending Forth

Benediction

> May God who is Alpha and Omega,
>> who is, and was, and who is to come,
>> fill you with faith and conviction.
> May the Risen One fill you with peace and joy,
>> that you may affirm your faith.
> May the Spirit be breathed upon you
>> and give you peace. Amen.

May 5, 2019

Third Sunday of Easter
Laura Jaquith Bartlett

Color

White

Scripture Readings

Acts 9:1-6, (7-20); Psalm 30; Revelation 5:11-14; John 21:1-19

Theme Ideas

From death to life, from despair to joy, from obstacle to clear path—over and over again these themes pop up in the good news of God's love for us. And yet we continue to trip on the obstacles, to wallow in despair, and to grieve what we see as the victory of death. But Jesus is still patiently waiting, showing us exactly where to put down our nets to reap the abundance of God's love, if only we are willing to follow him.

Invitation and Gathering

Centering Words (Ps 30, Acts 9, John 21)
We thought death was always the end of the story, until God showed us new life in the resurrection. We thought

enemies were always enemies, until God showed us
new love on the road to Damascus. We thought despair
was always paralyzing, until God showed us new hope
in bulging fish nets. What is God waiting to show us
today?

Call to Worship (Ps 30, Acts 9)

We have traveled from the horror of Good Friday
to the joy and celebration of Easter.
>**We will give thanks to you forever, O God.**

The Lord has turned our sorrow and sadness
into dancing and joy.
>**We will give thanks to you forever, O God.**

We come now to worship the one who transforms fear
into resurrection love.
>**We will give thanks to you forever, O God.**

Opening Prayer (Rev 5, Ps 30, John 21)

God of Life, we gather this day
>with the victory bells of Easter
>>still ringing in our ears.

We come joyfully this day
>to celebrate your power and glory,
>>your wisdom and might.

May we remain faithful to your call to follow Jesus,
>secure in your promise:
>>that life will triumph over death,
>>that hope will triumph over despair,
>>and that love will triumph over fear.

We lift our grateful hearts to you. Amen.

Proclamation and Response

Prayer of Confession (John 21, Acts 9, Ps 30)
Resurrected One, you have proven
that nothing can defeat the power of your love,
and yet we continue to nurture our doubts.
Time and again, you demonstrate your ability
to transform despair in our human story
into miraculous hope in your divine narrative,
and yet we make ourselves at home
in the pit of desolation.
Over and over, you patiently plant your seeds of joy,
and yet we continue to scoff
at the puny seedlings that sprout,
as if we've never before witnessed
the tenacity of your regenerative Spirit.
God, call us again to follow you.
Show us again the miracle of your abundance.
Lead us again from the depths of our fear
into the Easter light of your never failing love.
Amen.

Words of Assurance (Ps 30:2-3 NRSV)
Hear this song of praise that God's people
have been singing for thousands of years:
"O Lord my God, I cried to you for help,
and you have healed me.
O Lord, you brought up my soul from Sheol,
restored me to life from among those
gone down to the Pit."
God heals all wounds, rescues all sinners,
and forgives all debts.
Join the song of praise!

(This moves nicely into a short chorus or hymn stanza focusing on assurance.)

Passing the Peace of Christ (Acts 9, John 21)

We are Easter people; let us embody the joy of the resurrection as we greet one another in the name of Christ. Use these or similar words of greeting with energy and excitement: "Christ is offering new life to you."

Introduction to the Word (John 21, Acts 9)

(Ring a single handbell or singing bowl or finger chimes. After about a five-second pause, have two voices speak, preferably from different parts of the room.)
Listen!
Do you hear the Spirit moving in our midst?
(Bell or chime sounds.)
Listen!
Jesus is calling to us today.
(Bell or chime sounds.)
Listen!
**God's word of hope is about to be spoken
in this very room.**
(Bell or chime sounds.)
Listen!
**Open your ears, your eyes, and your hearts
to hear the word of God.**

Response to the Word (Ps 30, Acts 9, John 21)

(Here are three variations on a response, using "Joy Comes with the Dawn" by Gordon Light, found at #2210 in The Faith We Sing.*)*
1. (Briefly teach the ASL sign for "morning," which is easily found on YouTube. Have a soloist sing the stanzas, then the congregation sings the refrain, while signing "morning"

during measures 2, 4, 6, and 8–9. Be sure to have a couple of leaders model the signing throughout).

2. (Sing and sign the refrain as in variation 1, but instead of singing the stanzas, have the accompanist(s) improvise quietly underneath while a worship leader reads:)

Saul was breathing threats and murder, but an encounter with the living Christ turned his life around. Peter was the bumbling disciple who never seemed to get the concept, and who denied knowing Jesus—not once, not twice, but three times. An encounter with the Living Christ turned his life around. Each one of us has traveled the Damascus road with Saul. Each one of us has turned our back on Jesus. Each one of us has been in the pit of despair and grief. The living Christ is waiting, calling, ready to transform our lives. Are we willing to embrace Christ and greet the new dawn? (The reading is followed by the refrain again.)

3. (Have the congregation sing the entire song, preferably with a song leader. During the refrain, have dancers dance as the congregation sings.)

Thanksgiving and Communion

Offering Prayer (Acts 9, John 21)

Generous God, you have given us nothing less
than new life.
We pray that our thanksgiving and rejoicing
will find a home through our gifts to you.
In mission, in outreach, and in ministry,
may we live out resurrection hope each day
as we answer your call to feed your sheep.
With grateful hearts,
we pray in the name of the living Christ. Amen.

Sending Forth

Benediction (Ps 30, Acts 9, John 21)
Take off your sackcloth
and put on your dancing clothes!
God is your dance instructor and partner.
The Holy Spirit is playing the melody
of forgiveness and love,
and the living Christ is ready to turn your sadness,
your grief, and your fear
into a new life of rejoicing.
So dance out this door
and spread the story of transformation
to all the hurt, grieving, and despairing people
you meet.
God goes with you, always!
(Have the people respond with the refrain of "Lord of the Dance" (Sydney Carter) or use an instrumental setting of the tune as a postlude.)

May 12, 2019

Fourth Sunday of Easter, Festival of the Christian Home/Mother's Day
Deborah Sokolove

Color

White

Scripture Readings

Acts 9:36-43; Psalm 23; Revelation 7:9-17; John 10:22-30

Theme Ideas

Jesus is both the lamb of God and the good shepherd—guiding us toward the source of living water, and taking care of us even when we are afraid or beset by enemies. We can trust in the promise of salvation and eternal life when we follow Jesus and trust God's goodness and grace.

Invitation and Gathering

Centering Words (Ps 23, John 10)

Do I trust God's goodness wherever I go and whatever I do? Am I ready to follow Jesus, wherever he leads me?

Call to Worship (Ps 23, John 10)
The Holy One knows each sheep,
calling to us by name.
We hear the voice of Jesus,
calling us to follow him.
The Holy One sees our need,
feeding us with wisdom and truth.
We know the voice of Jesus,
leading us to goodness and peace.
The Holy one protects and guides us,
showing us the way to eternal life.
Let us worship our Shepherd,
who calls us here.

Opening Prayer (Ps 23, John 10)
God of love and goodness,
you lead us into pastures of plenty,
giving us food for our bodies
and nourishment for our souls.
You show us the source of salvation,
filling our hearts with the clean, fresh water
of your love.
You guide us on difficult paths,
comforting us with the assurance of eternal life
in your name.
Help us recognize your voice,
that we may be at peace in your presence,
even when we are afraid. **Amen.**

Proclamation and Response

Prayer of Confession (Ps 23, John 10)
God of compassion and grace,
you call us to follow you

and to listen to the sound of your voice.
But we want to go our own way,
listening only to the sound of our desires.
You give us food that will fill our souls,
and water that will satisfy our thirst for you.
Still, we wander away,
looking for greener grass in other places.
You long to comfort our wounds
and protect us from harm.
Forgive us when we run towards danger,
refusing to accept the good gifts you offer.

Words of Assurance (Ps 23, John 10)
Hear the Good News:
God's forgiveness is an endless fountain of love,
washing us in the waters of eternal life.
In the name of Christ, you are forgiven.
In the name of Christ, you are forgiven.
Glory to God. Amen.

Passing the Peace of Christ (Ps 23, John 10)
At rest in the dwelling place of God, let us greet one
another with signs of peace.
The peace of Christ be with you.
The peace of Christ be with you always.

Response to the Word (Ps 23)
Compassionate Shepherd, Source of living water,
Spirit of eternal life,
we give you thanks for guiding us
in the way we should go. **Amen.**

Thanksgiving and Communion

Offering Prayer (Ps 23, John 10)
Compassionate Shepherd, accept these gifts
as signs of our gratitude
for the generous gifts you give us—
gifts flowing from the eternal stream
of your grace. **Amen.**

Great Thanksgiving
Christ be with you.
And also with you.
Lift up your hearts.
We lift them up to God.
Let us give our thanks to the Holy One.
It is right to give our thanks and praise.

It is a right, good and joyful thing,
always and everywhere to give thanks to you,
who pours out healing and hope,
even in the presence of our enemies.
We give you thanks for clean water and good food,
for shelter and comfort when life is hard,
and for your promise of eternal life.

And so, with your creatures on earth
and all the heavenly chorus,
we praise your name and join their unending hymn:
Holy, holy, holy Lord, God of power and might,
heaven and earth are full of your glory.
Hosanna in the highest. Blessed is the one
who comes in the name of the Lord.
Hosanna in the highest.

Holy are you, and holy is your son, Jesus Christ,
>who taught his disciples to listen for his voice
>and to follow him,
>even when all hope seemed lost.
On the night in which he gave himself up,
>Jesus took bread, broke it and said:
>"Take, eat, all of you.
>This is my body, broken for you and for many.
>Whenever you eat it,
>do so in remembrance of me."
After supper, he took the cup, saying:
>"This is the cup of the new covenant,
>poured out for the healing of the world.
>Whenever you drink it,
>do so in remembrance of me."

And so, in remembrance of your mighty acts
in Jesus Christ, we proclaim the mystery of faith.
>**Christ has died.**
>**Christ is risen.**
>**Christ will come again.**

Pour out your Holy Spirit on us,
>and on these gifts of bread and cup.
Make them be for us the body and blood of Christ,
>that we might live in him and he in us,
>>for the sake of a broken and hurting world.
In the name of the one who gives us eternal life,
>we give our thanks and praise. Amen.

Sending Forth

Benediction (Ps 23, Rev 7, John 10)

Follow the voice of Jesus wherever he leads.
Trust that he will nourish and protect you,
    and fill you with the goodness of God's love.
In the name of the one who calls and guides us,
    let us go out to love and serve the world.
    Amen.

May 19, 2019

Fifth Sunday of Easter

Mary Scifres

[Copyright © Mary Scifes. Used by permission.]

Color

White

Scripture Readings

Acts 11:1-18; Psalm 148; Revelation 21:1-6; John 13:31-35

Theme Ideas

It's a new day. Every scripture on this Easter season Sunday calls us to new life, new outlook, new hope, and a new call to love. Revelation's promise of a new heaven and new earth is coupled with Jesus' commandment that we are to love one another as we have been loved by Christ. As Peter explains his vision that all things created by God are holy and pure, he launches a new vision of the early church, one that will include all who are open to the Spirit's powerful presence. That Spirit of inclusion is reflected in the psalmist's celebration that all of creation proclaims God's praise—a joyous portrayal of the new heaven and new earth promised in Revelation 21.

Invitation and Gathering

Centering Words (Rev 21, Ps 148)

This is a new day, full of promise and new life. Praise
God for this glorious gift!

Call to Worship (Acts 11, Ps 148, John 13)

Gathered as one, welcoming all,
   we worship as a community of love.
Gathered in love, giving thanks for life,
   we come to sing God's praises.

Opening Prayer (Acts 11, John 13)

Spirit of life, breathe new life within us.
Blow through our worship
      with your enlivening presence,
            and rise up in us with new hope.
Dwell in our community, in our church,
      and in our hearts this day,
            that your love may bind us together
            and sends us forth to serve.

Proclamation and Response

Prayer of Confession (Acts 11, John 13)

Risen Christ, rise in our hearts and in our lives.
Bring new life into our midst
      when death threatens our hope.
Expand our love within our communities
      when love is in short supply.
Grant mercy in our world
      when sin and shadows threaten the peace.

Resurrect us with your grace,
  and raise us up as new creations in your love,
    we are forgiven, accepted, and free.
With joyful gratitude, we pray. Amen.

Words of Assurance (Rev 21, John 13)
  Christ quenches our thirst for mercy,
    and feeds our hunger for grace.
  In the love of the risen Christ,
    we are resurrected with forgiveness and compassion;
    we are new creatures in a love that never ends.

Passing the Peace of Christ (Acts 11, John 13)
  Love each other, as Christ loves us. Turn to your neighbor to share signs of this love, so that all may know we are loved and welcome here.

Introduction to the Word
  Come to drink from the living water,
    and listen for the gospel of hope.

Response to the Word (Ps 148)
  Praise God from the heavens.
  Praise God on high.
  Praise God with the sun and the moon.
  Praise God with the stars in the sky.
  Praise God with the ocean and its creatures.
  Praise God with the birds of the air.
  Praise God with the mountains.
  Praise God on high!

Thanksgiving and Communion

Invitation to the Offering (John 13)
  Called to love, called to give, let us give generously of our hearts and our gifts.

Offering Prayer (Acts 11, John 13)
> Living God, send your Holy Spirit to bless these gifts
> > with your life and hope.
> Send your Holy Spirit upon us,
> > that we also may bring life and hope to others
> > > as we share our gifts in the world.
> Love through us, live through us,
> > that others may know your life-giving love. Amen.

Sending Forth

Benediction (Acts 11, John 13)
> With faith in the Risen Christ,
> > **we go forth to proclaim new life.**
> With the power of God's Holy Spirit,
> > **we go forth to serve.**
> With the love of God our Creator,
> > **We go forth to love.**

May 26, 2019

Sixth Sunday of Easter
Mary Sue Brookshire

Color

White

Scripture Readings

Acts 16:9-15; Psalm 67; Revelation 21:1-10, 22–22:5; John 14:23-29

Theme Ideas

As the season of Eastertide draws to a close, we anticipate Christ's ascension. Yet even as he prepares the disciples for his departure, he assures them of God's continuing presence with humanity. The texts from Revelation and John remind us that God makes God's home with us. When we welcome others into our homes in God's name, as Lydia did in the reading from Acts, we are welcoming God.

Invitation and Gathering

Centering Words (Acts 16, Rev 21, John 14)
God makes a home with us. Open the door of your heart and invite God to come and stay.

Call to Worship (Rev 21, John 14)

Listen to the voice that shouts:
God's dwelling is with us now.
In work and in play,
God makes a home with us.
In sorrow and celebration,
God makes a home with us.
Lift your voices in praise for this good news:
God's dwelling is with us now!

Suggested Opening Hymn

"God Is Here, As We Your People"

Opening Prayer (Acts 16, Rev 21, John 14)

Come, Holy Spirit, our constant Companion.
Remind us of all that our brother Jesus taught.
Refresh us with water from your life-giving stream,
and renew us with your heavenly peace.
Grant us visions of your new creation,
and draw us together as sisters and brothers.
Come, Holy Spirit; come and stay.

Proclamation and Response

Prayer of Confession (Rev 21, John 14)

Emmanuel, you promise to dwell with us
in all our humanness.
We desire to keep your word,
yet there are times when we fall short,
we lack courage, and our faith falters.
Despite your gift of peace,
we are troubled and afraid.
Forgive us when we close our hearts
and shut you out.

Save us from the idolatry of self-sufficiency,
and be with us as our God.

Words of Assurance (Rev 21)
These words are trustworthy and true:
God is making all things new, including us.
We are God's sons and daughters,
and through Christ, we are forgiven. Amen.

Passing the Peace of Christ (John 14)
God gives us the gift of peace, not as the world gives,
but as a deep peace that casts out fear. Greet one another
with the sign of God's peace.

Response to the Word (Acts 16)
Like our ancestors in faith,
we have listened to the good news proclaimed.
Through your Holy Spirit, O God,
strengthen us to embrace your word.

Thanksgiving and Communion

Offering Prayer (Rev 21)
Alpha and Omega, from beginning to end,
you are our God.
With your abundant love,
you bless us beyond measure.
In gratitude, we share these gifts
and ask that you use them and use us
to achieve your purposes.
May all your sons and daughters
receive the inheritance of your peace. Amen.

Sending Forth

Benediction (Acts 16, Rev 21, John 14)
Sons and daughters of God,
God dwells with us.
Go as God's people.
Keep God's word.
Embrace God's message.
Receive God's peace. Amen!

June 2, 2019

Seventh Sunday of Easter

B. J. Beu

Color

White

Scripture Readings

Acts 16:16-34; Psalm 97; Revelation 22:12-14, 16-17, 20-21; John 17:20-26

Theme Ideas

Today's scriptures show God's power to the world. Jesus calls the disciples to be one, not only with one another, but also with him. Through this unity of spirit, the world may know God's presence through the disciples' ministry. In Acts, Paul has the power to heal a girl suffering from demon possession—a healing that leads to transformation throughout the town, as people witness this miraculous act. The glory of God is proclaimed in both Psalm 97 and Revelation 22. God's glory is evident even to the heavens, so that the world may know God. This is the ministry to which the disciples are sent on Pentecost—the ministry of showing and proclaiming

God's glorious presence to the world. *(This may also be celebrated as Ascension Sunday, see page 128.)*

Invitation and Gathering

Centering Words (John 17)

While we hold onto things that divide us, Jesus' prayer is that we may all be one.

Call to Worship (Rev 22)

The Alpha and Omega says, "Come."
Let everyone who hears
come into God's presence.
The tree of life says, "Come."
Let those who seek eternal life
come to the root and the descendent of David,
our bright morning star.
The Spirit and the bride say, "Come."
Let everyone who is thirsty
come to the heavenly banquet
and drink from the wine of our salvation.
Come! Let us worship God together.

Opening Prayer (Ps 97, Rev 22, John 17)

Alpha and Omega,
you are the first and the last,
the beginning and the end of all things.
In you all things move and have their being.
Be present in our time of worship,
as you have been present
in every moment of our lives.
For your light dawns for the righteous,
and your joy blesses the upright in heart.

Stir our hearts within us,
    that we may feel the kinship we have we you
    and with one another.
This we pray through the power of your Spirit
    and the radiance of the bright morning star.
Amen.

Proclamation and Response

Prayer of Confession or Prayer of Yearning (Ps 97, Rev 22)
God of fire and lightning, Lord of thunder and storm,
    clouds and thick darkness surround you in glory.
Despite our pretense of self-assurance,
    we feel insignificant in your presence.
We yearn to have the courage of Paul and Silas,
    who spoke your truth to power,
        even when it cost them their freedom.
Somehow, fear always seems to hold us back.
We long to fulfill Jesus' prayer
    that we may be one with you and each other.
But our longing cannot overcome
    the divisions we cling to
        through our prejudices
            and our need to set ourselves apart.
Forgive us, Holy One.
Shake the heavens and awaken us
    from our dreams of separateness.
For your light dawns on the righteous,
    and your joy comes to the upright in heart.
Bless us with wisdom and truth,
    that we may be instruments of your grace
        and vehicles of your saving love. Amen.

Words of Assurance (Ps 97)
> Light has dawned upon us through Christ,
>> our bright morning star.
>
> Walk in the light and know the joy of forgiveness,
>> through the love of God,
>> the grace of Jesus Christ,
>> and the power of the Holy Spirit.

Passing the Peace of Christ (John 17)
> Christ's hope is that we may all be one. Let us answer this hope as we share signs of unity in the passing of the peace of Christ.

Response to the Word (Ps 97, Rev 22, John 17)
> Alpha and Omega, first and the last,
>> beginning and ending of all things—
>>> begin a new work in us this day,
>>>> as your word takes hold in our lives.
>
> Bind us together in a bond of love
>> that shakes the very foundations
>>> of all that keeps us from abiding in you,
>>> as you abide in us.

Thanksgiving and Communion

Offering Prayer (Acts 16)
> God of earthquake and lightning,
>> break open the prisons of our fears,
>>> as you free our hearts
>>>> to acts of loving generosity.
>
> Bless the gifts we offer you this day,
>> that all may behold your glory
>>> in the love of your people. Amen.

Communion Prayer (John 17)
God of earthquake and lightning,
your power pervades the universe.
Pour out your Spirit and Power
upon these gifts of bread and wine,
that they may be for us
your presence among us.
As your Spirit calls us to unity,
live in us and through us
in the power we see in your Son, Jesus.
Make us one with you, one with each other,
and one in ministry to the world. Amen.

Sending Forth

Benediction (Rev 22, John 17)
The one who invited us to come now sends us forth
to share the light of the bright morning star
with the world.
We go forth from this place,
but we never leave God's presence.
May the grace of the Lord be with us,
as we seek to fulfill Christ's hope
that we may all be one.
We go forth, empowered and strengthened,
to love and serve as one people of God.

June 2, 2019

Ascension Day
Ciona Rouse

Color

White

Scripture Readings

Acts 1:1-11; Psalm 47; Ephesians 1:15-23; Luke 24:44-53

Theme Ideas

Ascension Day is a time to recognize God's glory and rule over the earth. Jesus has been given power and dominion over all things. This Sunday, we can highlight this regal Jesus, our humble king of kings. The music and atmosphere of worship this day should reflect the reign of the ascended Christ over all things. It should also draw us to a place where we recognize that our calling comes from the most high—we must search for the hope to which God has called us. *(This may also be celebrated as the Seventh Sunday of Easter, see page 123.)*

Invitation and Gathering

Centering Words (Acts 1, Luke 24)
Wait to be clothed with power from on high. The one who ascended will come to us again, bringing new life and new hope. Wait.
(B. J. Beu)

Call to Worship (Ps 47)
Clap your hands! Shout for joy!
Our Lord reigns on the throne of glory!
We open our hearts to the ascended Lord,
who sits on the throne of glory!

Opening Prayer (Eph 1)
Lord of Lords,
illumine our hearts this day,
that we may feel your glory
and live into the hope
to which you have called us. Amen.

—Or—

Opening Prayer (Acts 1)
Unknowable God, on this most unsettling day,
you drew Jesus to your side—
promising his companions Spirit, power,
mission, and purpose;
calling his disciples to trust a future
that they could not yet see.
As we look to Jesus this day,
give us the same hope of Spirit, power,
mission, and purpose,
and call to trust a future
that we too are yet unable to see.

Guide us into your depths,
    that we may glimpse the Spirit
        already at work in our lives—
            revealing your truth
                and empowering us to bear witness
                to the risen Christ.
We pray this in the name of Jesus,
    your Mystery, your Wisdom, your Glory.
(Susan Blain)

Proclamation and Response

Prayer of Confession (Luke 24)
O Lord, we have not lived our lives
    as kingdom people.
We place our crowns
    on hopelessness, fear,
        and selfishness.
We are ruled by our schedules
    and our need for control.
We make kings of the things we acquire
    and queens of our immediate desires.
We forget that your kingdom
    draws near to us on earth,
        as it is in heaven.
Forgive us, we pray.
Come, Lord,
    and open in us
        the gates of your kingdom. Amen.

Words of Assurance (Luke 24)
The God of our Lord Jesus Christ
blesses us and calls us kingdom people.

In the name of the reigning Christ,
we are forgiven.
> **In the name of the reigning Christ,**
> **we are forgiven. Glory to God! Amen.**

Passing the Peace of Christ (Acts 1)
The glory of God reigns in each of us! Let the peace of Christ within you greet the peace of Christ in your neighbor.

Response to the Word (Eph 1)
The word of God speaks to our hearts.
(silent reflection)
The word of God speaks to our community.
(silent reflection)
The word of God speaks to our nation.
(silent reflection)
The word of God speaks to our world.
(silent reflection)
May God give us a spirit of wisdom and revelation
as we come to know Christ.
> **Lord, help us know the glorious hope**
> **to which you have called us**
> **through your word.**

Thanksgiving and Communion

Invitation to the Offering (Luke 24)
Gifted with the grace of God, and clothed with power from on high, let us now offer ourselves to the building of God's kingdom.

Offering Prayer (Luke 24)

Bless these gifts, O Lord of all,
that we might worship you with great joy,
and serve your people with great love.
In Christ's name, amen.

Invitation to Communion

Come to the table. It's an open feast.
Christ invites us all—
the rich and the poor,
the outcast and the honored,
Come to the gathering of sinners and saints.
Come to this blessed table where Christ reigns.
Come and taste the kingdom of God,
where all are welcome.

Prayer following Communion

Lord, you have given us peace,
and blessed us with a taste
of your heavenly banquet.
As we leave your table,
usher us into your kingdom,
now and forever. Amen.

Sending Forth

Benediction (Ps 47)

Clap your hands, all you people!
Sing to God with songs of joy!
Go forth praising God, who reigns on high!

June 9, 2019

Pentecost Sunday

Mary Scifres

[Copyright © Mary Scifres. Used by permission.]

Color

Red

Scripture Readings

Acts 2:1-21; Psalm 104:24-34, 35b; Romans 8:14-17; John 14:8-17, (25-27)

Theme Ideas

There is a unity of Spirit that pervades both the Pentecost experience and the lectionary scripture readings. The unity of a diverse group of people (Acts 2), the unity of all of Christ's followers adopted into one, united family (Romans 8), and the unity of love connecting both our Trinitarian God and our human community (John 14), are also echoed in the psalmist's celebration of creation's expectant praise.

Invitation and Gathering

Centering Words (Acts 2, John 14)

Gathered as one in the presence of the Holy Spirit, we gather in the unity of love.

Call to Worship (Acts 2, Rom 8, John 14)
The Spirit of Truth is moving…
pouring out prophetic possibilities for all to see.
The Spirit of Truth is speaking…
offering words of vision and hope.
The Spirit of Truth is with us…
weaving dreams of unity and love.

Opening Prayer (Acts 2, Rom 8, John 14)
Spirit of Truth, pour out your presence on us.
Cause wonders to occur as we dream your dreams
and see your visions.
Create unity and love
as you weave us together as one body of Christ,
one family of God,
and one community of justice and peace.

Proclamation and Response

Prayer of Confession (Acts 2, Rom 8)
Abba, Father, Parent of us all,
bind us together as your children.
Free us from the chains of division and divisiveness.
Unstop our blocked ears,
that we might listen and hear one another
with understanding and compassion.
Pour out unity and love so abundant,
through the power of your Holy Spirit,
that all resistance to a new
Pentecost community may be swept away.

Words of Assurance (Acts 2)
Everyone who calls on the name of God has been saved,
is being saved, and will be saved.

Passing the Peace of Christ (Acts 2, Rom 8, John 4)
>   In the unity of God's Holy Spirit, may we offer signs of
>   unity and love to one another as we share the peace of
>   Christ.

Introduction to the Word (Acts 2, Rom 8, John 4)
>   Wait! Do you notice something about this moment?
>   The Spirit is near, as near as our next breath.
>   Breathe! Do you notice something about this breath?
>   The Spirit is here, in our very breath—
>> ready to speak, ready to move,
>> ready to transform our lives.

Response to the Word (Acts 2, Rom 8)
>   God's adoption papers are prepared.
>   Are we ready to sign on the dotted line?
>   The Spirit's presence is with us, ready to send us forth.
>   Are we ready to go where the Spirit moves us to go?
>   *(A time of silence may follow these words of invitation.)*

Thanksgiving and Communion

Invitation to the Offering (Acts 2)
>   Bring your different gifts, your many languages, your
>   unique ways of offering yourself to God and God's
>   world. All of your gifts are welcome here, in whatever
>   way you are ready to offer them.

Offering Prayer (Acts 2, Rom 8)
>   Holy Spirit, bless the gifts we bring
>> with your powerful presence.
>   Through these gifts, bring new life, new hope,
>> new visions of life, new dreams of hope,

and new possibilities for unity and love
in our world.

Invitation to Communion (Acts 2, Rom 8)
Daughters and sons, young ones and old,
  celebrate this gift of life
  as we join in holy communion.
Come to receive the bread
  that reminds of our unity
  as one body of Christ.
Come to receive the new wine of God's Holy Spirit
  that flows through all us with unifying love.

Sending Forth

Benediction (Acts 2)
Even as the Spirit sends new visions and dreams,
  the Spirit sustains us with ancient power
  and renewed strength and love.
Even as the Spirit sends us forth,
  the Spirit goes with us to lead the way.

June 16, 2019

Trinity Sunday, Father's Day
B. J. Beu
[Copyright © B. J. Beu. Used by permission.]

Color

White

Scripture Readings

Proverbs 8:1-4, 22-31; Psalm 8; Romans 5:1-5; John 16:12-15

Theme Ideas

God takes delight in the works of creation. During the making of the inhabited world, Wisdom rejoiced before God, taking delight in the human race. The psalmist marvels that amidst the wonders of creation, human beings were created but a little lower than God. Paul boasts of our hope to share in God's glory through the love poured out to us in the Holy Spirit. And John declares that this same Spirit will lead us into all truth. On Trinity Sunday, we celebrate the fullness of God that leads us into the fullness of life.

Invitation and Gathering

Centering Words (Prov 8)

As God's delight, Wisdom rejoiced before the Lord as the heavens and the earth were brought forth. May we too find delight as Wisdom calls to us now.

Call to Worship (Ps 8)

O Lord, our God, how majestic is your name
in all the earth!
> **Your voice causes the seas to roar**
> **and the winds to howl.**
> **You have set your glory above the heavens.**
> **The moon and the stars sing your praises.**
What are human beings that you are mindful of us?
> **Who are we that you care for us?**
Yet you have made us a little lower than the angels.
> **You have crowned us with glory and honor.**
O Lord, our God, how majestic is your name
in all the earth!

Opening Prayer (Prov 8, Ps 8, John 16)

Holy Wisdom, Spirit of truth,
> we behold your glory in the starry heavens,
> > and your wonder in the earth and sea.
Who are we that you care for us so deeply?
Why do you love us so completely?
May we heed your clarion call
> to lead lives steeped in your wisdom,
> > and to take delight in all of your goodness.
Come into our lives
> and lead us into the fullness of your truth,
> > that our lives might glorify you
> > > in all that we say and do. Amen.

Proclamation and Response

Prayer of Confession or Prayer of Yearning (John 16)
 Spirit of truth, we long to take delight
  in the wisdom you would share with us,
   but it is often too much to bear.
 We yearn to joyfully receive the blessings
  that Wisdom seeks to bestow upon us,
   but we have trusted our own wisdom,
    turning away from the fullness of truth
    that you alone reveal.
 Forgive our inattention,
  and guide us into the sheer delight
   of bearing witness to your glory,
    that Wisdom may delight in us now
     as when the world was young. Amen.

Assurance of Pardon (Prov 8)
 When God fashioned us from the dust of the ground,
  Wisdom rejoiced before the Lord,
  delighting in the human race.
 Wisdom calls to bless us and delight in us now,
  not to curse us.
 Have hope and take heart.

Passing the Peace of Christ (John 16)
 Jesus promises to send us the Spirit of truth to guide us
 into all truth. May we express the truth of God's love
 in the Spirit, as we share the peace of Christ with one
 another this day.

Response to the Word (John 16)
 As we reflect upon the word of God,
  may the Spirit of truth bring us wisdom.

As we meditate on the ways that lead to life,
    may the gospel message come alive in our hearts.
As we live according to the word of God,
    may the Spirit of truth bless us with wisdom,
    that we might reflect God's glory.

—Or—

Response to the Word (Prov 8)
    Wisdom rejoices and delights in the Lord!
    How can we keep from singing?
    Wisdom dances and twirls before our God.
    How can we keep from dancing?
    Wisdom proclaims the glory of God.
    How can we keep from rejoicing?
    Wisdom rejoices and delights in the Lord!
    How can we keep from singing?

Thanksgiving and Communion

Offering Prayer (Ps 8)
    Sovereign God, you have set us as stewards
        over the works of your hands.
    May the offerings we bring you this day
        reflect the seriousness of your commission
            to be stewards of your gifts;
        may they be signs of our willingness
            to joyfully share your bounty with the world.
    Amen.

Sending Forth

Benediction (Prov 8, Ps 8, Rom 5, John 16)
> Go with the blessings of the Holy Spirit.
> **God's Spirit leads us into truth.**
> Go with the blessing of holy Wisdom.
> **God's Wisdom is our delight.**
> Go with the blessing of the Son of God.
> **God's inheritance fills us with joy.**
> Go with grace and peace.

June 23, 2019

Second Sunday after Pentecost, Proper 7
B. J. Beu
[Copyright © B. J. Beu. Used by permission.]

Color

Green

Scripture Readings

1 Kings 19:1-15a; Psalm 42; Galatians 3:23-29; Luke 8:26-39

Theme Ideas

Even in the midst of calamity, God is there. When Elijah was hunted and wanted to give up, angels nurtured him, and God gave him rest. The psalmist speaks of the longing of the human heart for God when events turn against us, and expresses confidence in God's help. Galatians celebrates freedom in Christ and the removal of all distinctions that society uses to judge some people as less worthy than others. And Luke recalls the story of Jesus freeing the strong man from the demons and the chains that bound him. God is always there to set us free, always there to bind up our wounds, always there to lift us above the hatred we find in the world.

Invitation and Gathering

Centering Words (1 Kgs 19)

God speaks most clearly in silence.

Call to Worship (Ps 42)

All who thirst, refresh yourselves
in the waters of the living God.
As a deer longs for flowing streams,
our souls long for God.
All who weep, comfort yourselves
in the safety of the living God.
As a deer longs for flowing streams,
our souls long for Christ.
All who feel lost and forgotten, find home and family
in the house of the living God.
As a deer longs for flowing streams,
our souls long for the Spirit.
Come! Revive yourselves
in the waters of the living God.

—Or—

Call to Worship (1 Kgs 19)

The wind buffets and blows,
cascading rocks down the mountainside.
Surely, God is in the wind?
The earthquake shakes and shatters,
shaking the very foundation of the earth.
Surely, God is in the earthquake?
The fire crackles and roars,
licking at the roots of life.
Surely, God is in the fire?
Where is God to be found?

Listen carefully...
God is here, in the sound of sheer silence.

Opening Prayer (1 Kgs 19)
God of mystery,
> open our eyes,
>> that we may see you in unfamiliar places;
> open our ears
>> that we may hear you speak
>>> in the sound of sheer silence;
> open our hearts,
>> that we may feel the depth of your love.
When we wander in the wilderness of fear and death,
> revive us with your care,
>> that we may find strength for our journey
>>> and return to the land of hope and life.
Amen.

Proclamation and Response

Prayer of Confession or Prayer of Yearning (1 Kgs 19, Luke 8)
Liberating God,
> in the midst of our brokenness,
>> we long to have you tend our needs,
>>> yet we resist your healing touch;
> in the midst of our confusion and doubt,
>> we yearn to lay down our worry and stress,
>>> yet we cling to old injuries
>>>> and righteous anger at perceived wrongs.
Free us from the chains that bind us,
> and help us embrace the true freedom you offer.
Heal us and nourish us, O God,

that we might see as Jesus sees,
and love as Jesus loves. Amen.

Assurance of Pardon (1 Kgs 19)

Even when we are full of despair like Elijah;
even when we want nothing more than to give up,
God sends angels to tend us and restore us to life.
Rejoice in the assurance that the one who calls us
is faithful.

Passing the Peace of Christ (Ps 42)

As a deer longs for flowing streams, our souls long for
the love of God. May we express this longing and the
love we find in God as we share the peace of the Lord
with one our sisters and brothers in Christ.

Scripture Litany or Response to the Word (1 Kgs 19 NRSV)

Elijah, afraid and running for his life,
was confronted by the living God at Mount Horeb.
"What are you doing here Elijah?
Go out and stand on the mountainside,
for the Lord is about to pass by."
Now there was a great wind—
a wind so strong that it split mountains
and broke rocks in pieces before the Lord.
But the Lord was not in the wind.
And after the wind, an earthquake shook the ground
to the roots of the mountain.
But the Lord was not in the earthquake.
And after the earthquake, a fire blazed up
toward the heavens.
But the Lord was not in the fire.
And after the fire, came a sound of sheer silence.
When Elijah heard it, he wrapped his face

in his mantle and went out and stood
at the entrance of the cave.
> **God speaks to us in silence.**
> **God is speaking still.**

Thanksgiving and Communion

Offering Prayer (1 Kgs 19, Luke 8)
Sovereign God,
>   you feed us by your own hand,
>   lest our souls shrivel
>   for want of nourishment;
>   you revive us with your waters of life,
>   lest our hearts faint
>   in the desert of our despair;
>   you call us back to life and new possibilities,
>   lest our hopes fail
>   in our sorrow and anguish.
Accept these offerings in gratitude and praise
>   for the many blessings
>   that we have received from your hand.
Accept the gift of our love,
>   and our pledge to love others
>   as you have loved us. Amen.

Sending Forth

Benediction (1 Kgs 19, Ps 42, Gal 3, Luke 8)
Go in the trust that God feeds our famished souls.
> **We go in the promise of God's love.**
Go in the assurance that Christ fills our lives
with hope for the future.

We go in the assurance of Christ's love.
Go in the freedom that the Spirit breaks the chains
that bind us.
We go in the freedom of the Spirit's love.
Go with God.

June 30, 2019

Third Sunday after Pentecost, Proper 8
B. J. Beu
[Copyright © B. J. Beu. Used by permission.]

Color

Green

Scripture Readings

2 Kings 2:1-2, 6-14; Psalm 77:1-2, 11-20; Galatians 5:1, 13-25; Luke 9:51-62

Theme Ideas

No matter how much we don't want it to happen, no matter how unprepared we feel to be on our own, mentors and guides eventually leave us, forcing us to carry on without them. Elisha follows Elijah until the very end—when his mentor and master is carried away in the whirlwind—for Elisha knows he cannot follow in the great prophet's footsteps without a double portion of Elijah's spirit. Jesus sets his face toward Jerusalem, knowing there is no return. The disciples will soon feel this loss. The psalmist cries out to God in distress, remembering God's great capacity to make everything right again. Galatians does not fit into this theme, but beautifully describes the fruit of the Spirit available to those who live by the Spirit. We see this fruit in the lives of Elijah, Elisha, and Jesus; indeed, we see it within our own lives when we love our neighbor as we love ourselves.

Invitation and Gathering

Centering Words (2 Kgs 2)
Do not fear fiery horses and chariots of fire, for they are signs of God's presence. Do not fear the whirlwind and acts of wonder, for they are signs that God draws near.

Call to Worship (2 Kgs 2, Luke 9)
God calls us to be people of the Spirit.
We are people of the whirlwind—
riding fiery horses and chariots of fire.
God calls us to be heirs with Christ.
We are heirs of freedom—
heirs of a love that will not let us go.
God calls us be children of the Most High.
We are children of promise—
people of God's glorious hope.
Come! Let us worship.

Opening Prayer or Prayer of Longing (2 Kgs 2, Ps 77, Luke 9)
Mighty God, your voice is like the crash of thunder;
    your breath is like a whirlwind
        that breaks the mighty cedars
            and levels everything in its path.
Come to us, Holy One,
    when we have need of you,
        for we feel abandoned and alone.

You alone can comfort us.
You alone can lead us through the waters
 of grief and loss.
You alone can help us reach other shores
 and find our way home.
As we gather to worship you this day,
 give us the courage to ask with Elisha
 for a double portion of your Spirit;
 for we can do nothing on our own.
In your faithful name, we pray. Amen.

Proclamation and Response

Prayer of Confession or Prayer of Yearning (Gal 5)
Gracious God, bestower of every good gift,
 we long to know true freedom in Christ
 and to taste the fruit of your Spirit,
 but we remain slaves to our baser instincts
 and are prisoners of our petty quarrels;
 we yearn to love our neighbor as ourselves
 and to know perfect forgiveness in that love,
 but we cling to old wounds
 and hold onto old injuries.
Help us claim our godly inheritance,
 that our lives may bear the fruit of your Spirit:
 love, joy, peace, patience, kindness, generosity,
 faithfulness, gentleness, and self-control;
 through Christ our Lord. Amen.

Words of Assurance (Gal 5)
Christ came to set us free, that we might have life
 and have it abundantly.

Live in the Spirit, and the Spirit will guide you
   in truth and grace.
Rejoice in the assurance of God's faithful love.

Passing the Peace of Christ (Gal 5)
   The fruit of the Spirit is peace. Share this peace with one
   another in joy and thanksgiving as we pass the pass the
   peace of Christ.

Response to the Word (Gal 5)
   The fruit of the Spirit is love, joy and peace.
      Give us this fruit always, O God.
   The fruit of the Spirit is patience, kindness,
   and generosity.
      Feed us with your Spirit, Holy One.
   The fruit of the Spirit is faithfulness, gentleness,
   and self-control.
      Lead us to life, Spirit of the living God.
   The fruit of the Spirit leads us home.
      Lead on, Spirit, for time is precious to us.

Thanksgiving and Communion

Offering Prayer (2 Kgs 2, Gal 5)
   You give us freedom to turn back, O Lord,
      when the road seems too difficult to travel.
   But when we have the strength to carry on
      and ask for a double portion of your Spirit,
         as Elisha before us,
            we find blessing upon blessing.
   May our offering reflect our gratitude
      for your many gifts—
         especially for the fruit of your Spirit.

May these gifts lift up others in their need,
 that they may have what they need to live
  and to find the freedom to choose life
   in its fullness. Amen.

Sending Forth

Benediction (Gal 5, Luke 9)
 Go forth from this place in the freedom of Christ
  and the transforming love of God.
 Go forth from our time of worship in the love of God
  and the fruit of the Holy Spirit.
 Relish the sweet taste of love, joy, peace, patience,
  kindness, generosity, faithfulness, and self-control.
 Go forth to love your neighbor as yourselves,
  and you will touch eternal life each and every day.

July 7, 2019

Fourth Sunday after Pentecost, Proper 9
Mary Scifres
[Copyright © Mary Scifres. Used by permission.]

Color

Green

Scripture Readings

2 Kings 5:1-14; Psalm 30; Galatians 6:(1-6), 7-16; Luke 10:1-11, 16-20

Theme Ideas

There is an elegant simplicity to the healing and ministry expressed in each of today's scriptures. Simply "wash and become clean," and Naaman is healed. "I cried out for help, and you healed me," the psalmist sings to God. The epistle advises, "Carry each other's burdens and you will fulfill the law of Christ." Jesus instructs disciples to simply offer God's peace from house to house. No advanced training, no fancy words, and no elaborate rituals are required as we answer God's call to serve and to heal the world.

Invitation and Gathering

Centering Words *(2 Kgs 5, Gal 6, Luke 10)*
    Bring peace. Bring healing. God's kingdom is near.

Call to Worship *(2 Kgs 5, Ps 30, Gal 6, Luke 10)*
    Sing praise to God,
    who changes our mourning to dancing.
        Sing praise to Christ,
        who offers healing to our sickness.
    Sing praise to the Spirit,
    who brings peace to our turmoil.
        Sing praise to God,
        who gives us strength for the journey.
    Singing God's praises,
        we come to worship and pray.

Opening Prayer *(2 Kgs 5, Ps 30, Gal 6, Luke 10)*
    Healer God, bring your shalom
        to our time of worship.
    Weave your peace and your healing
        through our words and our thoughts this day.
    Flow through us with your presence and your love,
        that we may bring your presence and your love
            to all the world.
    In hope and gratefulness, we pray.

Proclamation and Response

Prayer of Confession *(2 Kgs 5, Ps 30, Gal 6, Luke 10)*
    O Great Physician, we cry out in our sickness
        for healing and hope.

We look for your peace,
    even in our troubled world.
We yearn for your grace,
    even in our sinful moments.
We need you more than ever,
    even as you need us.
Bring healing; bring peace;
    bring grace; bring strength,
        that we may serve and love your world,
        even as serve and love us so generously.

Words of Assurance (Ps 30, Luke 10)

God has dressed us in joy,
    blessing us with grace and mercy.
God turns our mourning into dancing
    and offers us the peace that passes all understanding.

Passing the Peace of Christ (Luke 10)

In the miraculous peace of Christ, may we share the miracle of peace and love with one another.

Prayer of Preparation (Gal 6)

God of mercy and peace, open our eyes
    to see your presence in the faces gathered here.
Open our ears this day
    to hear your wisdom in the words that are spoken.
Open our hearts and minds
    to recognize your guidance,
        not only in this time of worship,
        but in all the moments of our lives.

Response to the Word (2 Kgs 5, Ps 30, Gal 6, Luke 10)

With what shall we journey in faith?
Not with bags or sandals.

Nor with rituals or rules.
No, but with blessings of peace.
With acts of mercy.
With words of love.
With prayers of healing.
For all who are willing to receive.
With peace, mercy, love and healing,
we are ready to journey with God.

Thanksgiving and Communion

Invitation to the Offering (Gal 6)
As we offer our gifts, we are reminded of Christ's call to carry one another's burdens. May those of us with abundance give abundantly. May those of us in great need receive abundantly. And may all of our gifts be an abundant blessing to God.

Offering Prayer (2 Kgs 5, Ps 30, Gal 6, Luke 10)
Loving God, with these gifts,
bring healing and hope
where illness and despair prevail.
Bring peace into the warring madness of our world,
and shine the light of your love
into the places and people haunted by hatred.
Loving God, transform these gifts
and each of these givers,
that they may be your loving presence
and your healing in the world. Amen.

Sending Forth

Benediction

Take nothing for the journey,
but go on the journey anyway.

**We will go on journeys of service, love,
and peace.**

Take nothing for the journey,
but follow Christ to the end.

We go to bring Christ's presence to the world.

July 14, 2019

Fifth Sunday after Pentecost, Proper 10
Mary Petrina Boyd

Color

Green

Scripture Readings

Amos 7:7-17; Psalm 82; Colossians 1:1-14; Luke 10:25-37

Theme Ideas

A concern for justice weaves through these passages, with a particular concern for the poor and needy. Amos sees the plumb line and knows that the nation is judged; God speaks to the psalmist commanding justice for the needy; in Colossians, Paul prays that the people live fruitful lives; and most powerfully, Jesus answers the question, "Who is my neighbor?" with the parable of the good Samaritan. In this teaching, the despised outsider, not the religious officials, cares for one beaten and left for dead. To follow Jesus is to respond to needs wherever they arise with compassion and practical help.

Invitation and Gathering

Centering Words (Col 1)
Faith, love, and hope are gifts of God.
They grow and bear the fruit of grace and compassion.

Call to Worship (Col 1)
We gather as God's people.
God has given us faith and hope.
God's message of love is with us.
We are growing in the knowledge of God.
God calls us out of darkness and into the light.
We give thanks with joy to our God!

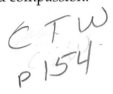

Opening Prayer (Col 1, Luke 10) INVOCATION
Holy One, we gather as your people,
giving thanks that we can be together
to hear your word, offer our prayers,
and sing your praises.
Draw us together in your love,
that we may know you more deeply.
Open our hearts to a deeper understanding of your will,
and work within our lives,
that we may produce the fruit of compassion.
Amen.

Proclamation and Response

Prayer of Confession (Amos 7, Col 1, Luke 10)
God, we want to measure up to your hopes for us.
Open our eyes to see the places in our world
where our compassion can help.

Give us loving hearts,
    that we might reach out to our neighbors
      when they are in need.
Grant us the courage to take risks
    for the sake of your kingdom.
Help us to live lives that are worthy of you. Amen

Words of Assurance (Col 1)
God sets us free through Jesus,
    and forgives our sins.
We live in the light of God's love.

Passing the Peace of Christ (Col 1)
Grace and peace to you. Grace and peace to one another.
Grace and peace to the world. Let us share this peace
today as we pass the peace of Christ.

Prayer of Preparation (Col 1)
Holy God, Living Word,
    you give us this message
      to show us your will.
May the good news grow within us,
    that we may be filled with wisdom,
      spiritual understanding,
        and the knowledge of God. Amen.

Response to the Word (Luke 10)
How shall we live?
    We will love the Lord our God with all our heart,
    with all our being, and with all our mind.
How shall we love?
    We will love our neighbor as ourselves.
Who is our neighbor?
    Our neighbor lies by the road in pain.
    Our neighbor goes to bed hungry.
    Our neighbor has lost hope.

How shall we love our neighbor?
We will respond with love and compassion.
We will do what is needed to help others.
We will care for one another.

Thanksgiving and Communion

Invitation to the Offering (Luke 10)
"Go and do likewise," Jesus told the lawyer. We are called to love our neighbors, giving of our time and money. There are many ways to be a good Samaritan.

Offering Prayer (Ps 82, Col 1, Luke 10)
Creating God, thank you for your world of beauty,
abundance, and blessing.
Use our gifts to bring justice and healing to all people.
As we offer our gifts,
we also offer our lives in your service,
that we may do your will. Amen

Sending Forth

Benediction (Col 1, Luke 10)
Go to live lives worthy of God.
When you stumble upon places of pain and struggle,
don't cross the street and walk past...
reach out in love.
Know that the seed of God's Spirit grows in your lives,
yearning to bear the fruit of justice and compassion.
Go with God's grace and peace.

July 21, 2019

Sixth Sunday after Pentecost, Proper 11
Karin Ellis

Color

Green

Scripture Readings

Amos 8:1-12; Psalm 52; Colossians 1:15-28; Luke 10:38-42

Theme Ideas

Our scriptures begin with harsh words from the prophet Amos. God proclaims there will be famine, lamentation, and even baldness because the people have forgotten who and whose they are. The psalmist echoes these thoughts, but ends with a word of hope. The promise of God's steadfast love is never far from the lips of the psalmist. Both the epistle and the Gospel of Luke remind us to put Christ first. When we do this, our daily troubles and tasks are diminished because we come to know the glory and wisdom of the Lord through Christ. All of these scriptures remind us to look to God first and to prioritize God's ways in our lives.

Invitation and Gathering

Centering Words (Luke 10)

This is a place to pause from the hustle and bustle of our days. This is a time to listen to the spoken word, enjoy the notes of a song, find joy in the face of our neighbor, and dwell in the Spirit of God.

Call to Worship (Amos 8, Luke 10)

Come, all who are burdened with many tasks.
God provides a space for rest and renewal.
Come, all who have turned away from God.
God welcomes us with healing and forgiveness.
Come, all who desire to know Christ.
**Here we find unexpected grace
and unconditional love.
Thanks be to God!**

Opening Prayer (Ps 52, Luke 10)

Creator of all, we come from many places.
Some of us come with heavy hearts.
Some of us come with questions and few answers.
Some of us come with joys bursting from our souls.
Some of us come with long "to do" lists.
Help us lay aside all that we carry with us
    and focus on you—
        the source of our lives,
        the one who fills our days with joy and love,
        the one who provides answers to our questions.
Almighty God, we come this day
    to turn our minds and hearts toward you.
In the name of Christ, we pray. Amen.

Proclamation and Response

Prayer of Confession (Amos 8)

Great God, our source of comfort and hope,
> we do not always follow your ways.

We forget to put you first in our lives.

We forget to abide by the rules of living
> you have set before us.

We hurt each other and ignore the needs
> of those around us.

We become complacent in our quest for justice.

Yet, even when we are unfaithful to you,
> you remain faithful to us.

Your steadfast love holds and heals us,
> no matter where we are
> > or what we have done.

Help us turn our lives toward you,
> not only on this day,
> > but every day.

In your merciful name, we pray. Amen.

Words of Assurance (Ps 52:8 NRSV)

The psalmist proclaims,
> "I trust in the steadfast love of God
> forever and ever."

Brothers and sisters, receive forgiveness,
> and trust that God's love is always with us. Amen.

Passing the Peace of Christ (Col 1)

God chose to have Christ dwell in each of us. You are invited to turn to one another, share peace with one another, and discover the glory of Christ in your neighbor.

Prayer of Preparation (Luke 10)
    Loving Christ, may this be a time
        when we lay aside everything else
            to come before you and listen to your word.
    May our minds, our energy, and our hearts
        be focused on you. Amen.

Response to the Word (Col 1, Luke 10)
    Light of our lives, we know that words are powerful.
    May the words we have heard
        move in our hearts in such a way
            that we are compelled to look toward you
                and live in your ways. Amen.

Thanksgiving and Communion

Invitation to the Offering (Amos 8)
    Sometimes the blessings in our lives overflow like a basket of summer fruit. Other times the blessings are not as abundant. Whether our basket is full or meager, let us offer to God what we can in order to show our thanksgiving and praise.

Offering Prayer (Col 1)
    Source of all that is, we offer these gifts to you.
    We give what we can
        and ask that you bless and multiply our offering,
            so that our brothers and sisters near and far
                may know your abundant love
                    and your tender mercy.
    We also offer you our very selves.

Through our lives,
may people everywhere come to know
the glory and wisdom we have found in Christ.
In your holy name, we pray. Amen.

Sending Forth

Benediction (Col 1, Luke 10)
Sisters and brothers, as you leave this place,
take time to be with Christ so that you may know
the blessings of our God.
And now may the peace of God, the love of Christ,
and the comfort of the Holy Spirit
be with you now and always.

July 28, 2019

Seventh Sunday after Pentecost, Proper 12
B. J. Beu
[Copyright © B. J. Beu. Used by permission.]

Color

Green

Scripture Readings

Hosea 1:2-10; Psalm 85; Colossians 2:6-15, (16-19); Luke 11:1-13

Theme Ideas

The contrast among today's scriptures is not uncommon in the ordinary season. One theme is to center on Hosea's depiction of the absolute devastation of losing touch with God and with God's call in our lives. The psalmist echoes this feeling of abandonment, but recalls God's steadfast love and God's promise of hope and renewal. The epistle challenges the community of faith to embrace the promises of God; it likewise challenges individuals within these communities to continue growing on their journeys of faith. Finally, the Gospel contains the Lord's Prayer and the encouragement to seek the Lord— for those who seek, find; and those who ask, receive.

Invitation and Gathering

Centering Words (Luke 11)

re-too for CTW

Seek, and you will find. Knock, and the door will be opened for you. Ask, and it will be given to you.

Call to Worship (Ps 85, Luke 11)

Come to worship the God of our salvation.
God's goodness has called us here.
Seek, and you will find.
With joy, we sing of Christ's steadfast love.
Knock, and the door will be opened for you.
Here, steadfast love and faithfulness meet.
Ask, and it shall be given to you.
Here, righteousness and peace kiss.
Come to worship the God of our salvation.
God's goodness has called us here.

Opening Prayer (Luke 11)

Sustaining God, grant us this day
the blessings of your faithfulness
and your grace.
Where there is hunger,
give us bread.
Where there is thirst,
give us cool water to drink.
Where there is loneliness,
give us friendship.
Forgive our transgressions and our errant ways,
as we forgive those who transgress against us.
Where we have wronged another,
guide us into reconciliation.
And where we have been wronged,

guide us on the journey of forgiveness.
For yours is the kingdom and the power
and the glory forever. Amen.

Proclamation and Response

Prayer of Confession or Prayer of Yearning (Ps 85, Luke 11)
How long, O Lord, will you hide your face from us?
As our world is ripped apart,
    we long for the day of your salvation.
As our lives are tattered and torn,
    we yearn for you to restore our fortunes.
As we knock on the door and seek your face,
    open the door to us,
        for we need your presence
            if we are to be whole once more.
Show us your steadfast love, Holy One.
Fulfill your promise to answer our prayers,
    and we will dwell with joy
        in your house forever. Amen.

Words of Assurance (Luke 11)
The one who gives us our daily bread each day,
    blesses us with what we need
    each and every day of our lives.
The one who forgives our sins
    answers our prayers and offers us fullness of life.
    Thanks be to God!

Passing the Peace of Christ (Ps 85)
In the Spirit, steadfast love and faithful meet; righteousness and peace kiss. Let us share signs of the Spirit's gifts as we pass the peace of Christ.

Response to the Word (Col 2)
>Receive the word of God.
>Breathe the truth of Christ's love.
>Lift your weary limbs,
>>and let the Spirit blow through your lives.
>Open your eyes to the gift of renewal and grace.

Thanksgiving and Communion

Offering Prayer (Ps 85)
>God of manifold blessings,
>>surely your salvation is at hand.
>In your Spirit, steadfast love and kindness meet;
>>righteousness and peace kiss.
>For your unfailing faithfulness,
>>we give you thanks and praise.
>Receive the gifts we return to you now,
>>that through our tithes and offerings
>>>all people may know your goodness
>>>and your grace. Amen.

Sending Forth

Benediction (Ps 85, Col 2)
>Go forth as God's faithful ones,
>showing love and kindness to all.
>>**We will scatter seeds of righteousness and peace,**
>>**that God's kingdom may bloom anew.**
>Go forth and grow strong with Christ as the root
>and the foundation of your lives.
>>**We will bloom in the faith God has given us—**
>>**a faith that springs forth to bless the world.**
>Go with God.

August 4, 2019

Eighth Sunday after Pentecost, Proper 13
Deborah Sokolove

Color

Green

Scripture Readings

Hosea 11:1-11; Psalm 107:1-9, 43; Colossians 3:1-11; Luke 12:13-21

Theme Ideas

God loves us and gives us good gifts. It saddens God when we deceive and abuse one another, when we are greedy or jealous or violent, and when we live without love and compassion. When we live in gratitude for all that we have received, and when we place our trust in God rather than in material things, we die to our old selves and become one in Christ, so that we may serve the world.

Invitation and Gathering

Centering Words (Col 3)

We are all one in Christ, wherever we come from and whatever we look like. Give thanks to God for granting us eternal life.

Call to Worship (Ps 107)

God calls to us from the wilderness of our lives.
We cry out to God to save us
from all that we fear.
God satisfies all who hunger,
and gives water to all who thirst.
We hunger and thirst for God.
Come and give thanks, for God is good.
We come to worship the God who calls us.

Opening Prayer (Hos 11, Col 3, Luke 12)

Loving, generous God,
long ago you called your people out of Egypt,
teaching them to live in peace with one another
in the wilderness.
When they settled in the land you gave them,
they saddened you by worshipping idols,
putting their trust in material goods,
cheating and lying and acting with violence
instead of with love.
When Jesus told them of your open-hearted grace,
they saddened him with their greed and jealousy,
and their desire to have him judge between them.
Today, you call us to remember
that we have died and risen in Christ.
You challenge us to put away our anger and fears,
an to trust that you will always fill us
with good things.
Help us strip away all that keeps us
from clothing ourselves in Christ,
that we may be your people,
showing your love to all of your creation.
Amen.

Proclamation and Response

Prayer of Confession (Hos 11, Ps 107, Col 3, Luke 12)
Generous, compassionate God,
you call us to live in peace with one another,
sharing the good gifts you give us
with all of your creation.
Yet, we hang on tightly to our possessions,
fearing that we will not have enough.
You call us to remember that we are one in Christ,
and to treat one another with love and respect.
Still, we argue over little things,
expecting you to tell us that we are right
and that others are wrong.
You call us to rely on you,
and to put our trust in your eternal love.
Forgive us when we turn away from you.

Words of Assurance (Ps 107)
God has promised to fill us with good things,
to satisfy our hunger and thirst with love and grace.
In the name of Christ, you are forgiven.
In the name of Christ, you are forgiven.
Glory to God. Amen.

Passing the Peace of Christ (Col 3)
Having clothed ourselves in Christ, let us greet one another with signs of peace.
The peace of Christ be with you.
The peace of Christ be with you always.

Response to the Word (Col 3)
Compassionate, loving God,
we give you thanks
for making us one in Christ;

we give you praise for pouring out your good gifts
on us and on all the world. Amen.

Thanksgiving and Communion

Offering Prayer (Hos 11, Luke 12)
Generous, compassionate God,
    accept these tokens of our gratitude
        for your many gifts.
Bless them that they may go forth
    and bless the world. **Amen.**

Great Thanksgiving
Christ be with you.
    And also with you.
Lift up your hearts.
    We lift them up to God.
Let us give our thanks to the Holy One.
    It is right to give our thanks and praise.

It is a right, good and joyful thing,
    always and everywhere, to give thanks to you.
As you gave our ancestors in faith
    food and water in the desert,
        even when they turned away from you,
        you have promised to free us from all divisions
        and to give us eternal life.

And so, with your creatures on earth
    and all the heavenly chorus,
        we praise your name and join their unending hymn:
    Holy, holy, holy Lord, God of power and might,
        heaven and earth are full of your glory.

**Hosanna in the highest. Blessed is the one
who comes in the name of the Lord.
Hosanna in the highest.**

Holy are you, and holy is Jesus, your anointed one,
    who taught us to beware
    of trusting earthly treasures
    and warned us to put our trust in you alone.

On the night in which he gave himself up,
    Jesus took bread, broke it, saying:
    "Take, eat, all of you.
    This is my body, broken for you.
    Whenever you eat it,
    do so in remembrance of me."
After supper, he took the cup, saying:
    "This is the cup of the new covenant,
    poured out for the healing of the world.
    Whenever you drink it,
    do so in remembrance of me."

And so, in remembrance of your mighty acts
    in Jesus Christ, we proclaim the mystery of faith.
    **Christ has died.
    Christ is risen.
    Christ will come again.**

Pour out your Holy Spirit on us,
    and on these gifts of bread and cup.
Make them be for us the body and blood of Christ,
    that we may be one in Christ,
        no longer divided by race or country
        or any other earthly sign.

For all these gifts,
we give our thanks and praise. **Amen**

Sending Forth

Benediction (Col 3)

Having clothed ourselves in Christ,
let us be Christ to a world
that hungers and thirsts for love.
In the name of the great giver of life,
the one who is life itself and the breath of life;
go in peace to love and serve the world.
Amen.

August 11, 2019

Ninth Sunday after Pentecost, Proper 14

B. J. Beu

[Copyright © B. J. Beu. Used by permission.]

Color

Green

Scripture Readings

Isaiah 1:1, 10-20; Psalm 50:1-8, 22-23; Hebrews 11:1-3, 8-16; Luke 12:32-40

Theme Ideas

Isaiah, the psalmist, and Luke make clear that worshiping the "right way," when our actions are contrary to the ways of justice and righteous, is spiritually empty and not pleasing to God. When we simply go through the motions in worship, God will not listen to the prayers of those who trample the weak and whose hands are full of blood. The psalmist echoes this sentiment, adding that our God is a devouring fire, and those who do not repent of their sinful ways will be utterly swept away. Still, those who go the right way will see the salvation of their God. In Luke, Jesus tells us not to worry, for it is God's pleasure to give us the kingdom. Still, Jesus warns that

we should store up treasures in heaven, not on earth—
for where our treasure is, there our hearts will be also.

Invitation and Gathering

Centering Words (Luke 12)
Do not be afraid little flock, it is God's good pleasure to
give you the kingdom.

—Or—

Centering Words (Luke 12:34 NRSV)
"Where your treasure is, there your heart will be also."

Call to Worship (Ps 50, Luke 12)
From the rising of the sun to its setting…
God speaks, summoning us.
In the perfection of the beauty all around us…
God shines forth, illuminating our hearts.
Those who bring thanksgiving as their sacrifice,
and those who go the right way, honor God.
They shall receive salvation from our God.
Those who worship God with acts of love and mercy…
God is pleased to give them the kingdom.
Come! Let our worship be justice and righteousness.

Opening Prayer (Isa 1, Luke 12)
Mighty God, dress us for action
in a world that needs us to care.
You promise that if we turn from our selfish ways,
we shall eat of the good of the land,
but if we refuse and rebel,
we will reap what we sow.
Your care and compassion call to us.

Your mercy and grace reach out to us.
We know it is your good pleasure
   to give us the kingdom.
As we light candles for worship,
   light your passion within us,
      that our true worship may be acts of justice
      and works of righteousness. Amen.

Proclamation and Response

Prayer of Confession or Prayer of Yearning (Isa 1, Luke 12)
   Forgive us, O God, when our prayers and devotions
      are divorced from works of love and justice.
   We long to be washed with your grace,
      and cleansed in your mercy.
   We yearn to store up treasure in heaven
      where no thief comes and no moth destroys,
         but we balk at the idea of selling our possessions
         and giving alms to the poor.
   We seek to remove the evil we harbor in our hearts,
      but it is a struggle to do good all the time.
   Transform our deeds of shame
      into acts of righteousness.
         that we might be instruments of your mercy
         and bearers of your compassion and grace.
   In your holy name, we pray. Amen.

Words of Assurance (Isa 1, Luke 12)
   Don't be afraid, little flock,
      for God delights in giving us the kingdom.
   Through the Spirit of the living God,
      we are washed clean and made whole;
      we receive the treasure of God's mercy and love!

Passing the Peace of Christ (Luke 12)
> It is God's good pleasure to give us the kingdom. Let us share the treasure of love and mercy with one another as we pass the peace of Christ.

Introduction to the Word (Isa 1, Ps 50)
> Hear the word of the Lord
> > and listen to God's teaching.
>
> For God's word contains warning and promise—
> > a gift to be treasured and lived.
>
> Whether we receive this gift is a choice we make.

Response to the Word (Isa 1, Luke 12)
> Let us be ready...
> > **Our God comes at unexpected times**
> > **and in unexpected places.**
>
> Let us dress for action...
> > **God has work for us**
> > **and requires our hands and feet,**
> > **as well as our hearts and minds.**
>
> Let us dress with love and compassion...
> > **God asks us to keep our lamps lit**
> > **and to be the light of the world.**
>
> Let us be ready...

Thanksgiving and Communion

Invitation to the Offering (Luke 12)
> Where our treasure is, there our hearts will be also. As we collect our tithes and offering, let us bring the treasure of our love.

Offering Prayer (Luke 12)
    God of grace and God of glory,
        as we offer these earthly treasures back to you,
            transform our gifts into your love and mercy
                by the power of your Holy Spirit.
    May these gifts be signs that our true treasure
        is from above—
            the treasure of justice and righteousness
                for your children everywhere. Amen.

Sending Forth

Benediction (Luke 12)
    People get ready.
        We are dressed for love.
    People get ready.
        We are dressed for service.
    People get ready.
        We are dressed for mercy and compassion.
    People get ready.
        We are dressed to shine the light of Christ.
    Go ... for you are dressed as children of God.

August 18, 2019

Tenth Sunday after Pentecost, Proper 15
B. J. Beu
[Copyright © B. J. Beu. Used by permission.]

Color

Green

Scripture Readings

Isaiah 5:1-7; Psalm 80:1-2, 8-19; Hebrews 11:29–12:2; Luke 12:49-56

Theme Ideas

Isaiah and the psalmist proclaim that God lovingly plant- ed the vineyard Israel, but its walls have fallen and the vineyard is being destroyed. But while Isaiah claims that this is God's doing in response to Israel's injustice and bloodshed, the psalmist holds out hope that God will yet save the people and give them new life. Hebrews im- plores us to follow the great cloud of witnesses who have set aside the weight of sin and death, that we may look to Christ, the perfecter of our faith. In Luke, Jesus yearns to bring fire to the earth to bring true judgment to all. God is not just the one who plants us like a vineyard, God is the one who destroys the vineyards that bears bad fruit. And yet, it is this same God, in the midst of our destruction, to whom we look for our salvation—salvation through fire and baptism. The great cloud of witnesses testifies to our need to follow Christ, who is our hope.

Invitation and Gathering

Centering Words (Ps 80, Luke 12)

Jesus came to bring the fire to the earth—the fire of the Holy Spirit. We will either be baptized by this fire or be consumed by it. Those who have ears to hear, let them hear.

Call to Worship (Isa 5, Ps 80, Heb 11)

The one who planted us as a vineyard,
the one who protects us with the walls of love,
calls us here.
As the plantings of God's justice,
we come to bear the fruit of righteousness,
and to protect the poor from violence
and bloodshed.
The one who tills the soil of our spirit
roots us in Christ, the perfecter of our faith.
As the plantings of God's hope,
may we flourish in the soil of God's joy,
joining the great cloud of witnesses before us.
The one who tends our hearts and souls as a vineyard
sustains us by the rains of God's Spirit.
As the plantings of God's love and mercy,
may we grow healthy and strong,
bearing the fruit of salvation.
Come! Let us worship.

—*Or*—

Call to Worship (Heb 11, Luke 12)
This is the place where saints worship.
This is the place where we are baptized
with the fire of the Holy Spirit.
This is the place where faith abounds.
This is place where doubts are welcome.
This is the place where Christ perfects us.
This is a place where the Spirit completes us.
Come worship with the saints
and be baptized by the fire of the Holy Spirit.

Opening Prayer (Isa 5, Ps 80)
God of the vineyard,
plant your passion for justice and righteousness
in the soil of our lives;
prune our thirst for bloodshed and strife
from the wild growth of self-interest and greed.
Nurture us in this time of worship,
and make room in our hearts
for compassion and generosity,
Help us bear good fruit and live as your people—
a people of passion for justice and righteousness.
Amen.

Proclamation and Response

Prayer of Confession or Prayer of Yearning (Isa 5, Luke 12)
Bountiful God, you have sheltered us
inside the walls of your loving care.
We long to be the good grapes of your planting,
but we have yielded the wild grapes
of our own willful ways.
We yearn to bear the fruit of justice and righteousness,

but we have neglected the poor among us
and have ignored the weighty matters of the law.
Prune away our self-centered ways
and dress us with your forgiveness.
Call down the fire of your baptism,
that we may be born anew
in the ashes of your refiner's fire. Amen.

Words of Assurance (Heb 11)
When we look to Christ,
the pioneer and perfecter of our faith,
we learn to love others as Christ has loved us;
we find wholeness and forgiveness.

Passing the Peace of Christ (Luke 12)
The peace that Christ brings comes through the fire of
the Holy Spirit. Let us share the peace that sets our souls
on fire as we pass the peace of Christ.

Response to the Word (Heb 11)
Since we are surrounded by so great a cloud of witnesses,
let us set aside every weight and obstacle
that keeps us from running the race
set before us;
let us look to Jesus, the pioneer and perfecter
of our faith.

Thanksgiving and Communion

Offering Prayer (Isa 5, Ps 80)
Faithful God,
your love for us is like sunlight
that blesses young vines in a vineyard;

your passion for our salvation is like rain
that kisses the ground of our being
to bring forth life.
With joy for your bounty,
we bring our gifts before you this day,
that your vineyard may increase,
through the care of our labor
and the treasure of our purse. Amen.

Sending Forth

Benediction (Isa 5, Luke 12)
Go forth and bear the fruit of justice and righteousness.
We go to bear the fruit of God's vineyard.
Go forth and bear the fruit of mercy and peace.
We go to bear the fruit of Christ's grace.
Go forth and bear the fruit of hope and joy.
We go to bear the fruit of the Holy Spirit.
Go forth and bear the fruit of the kingdom of God.

August 25, 2019

Eleventh Sunday after Pentecost, Proper 16
Mary Scifres
[Copyright © Mary Scifres. Used by permission.]

Color

Green

Scripture Readings

Jeremiah 1:4-10; Psalm 71:1-6; Hebrews 12:18-29; Luke 13:10-17

Theme Ideas

Today's scriptures remind us to listen for God's miraculous presence—whether God's voice comes as a call to ministry (Jeremiah 1:9-10), a promise of salvation (Psalm 71:3), a prophetic warning and promise (Hebrews 12:22-29), or a word of healing (Luke 13:12). Recognizing God's presence in our lives opens new avenues for life and growth, if only we open our minds to hear and receive the messages sent from God.

Invitation and Gathering

Centering Words (Jer 1, Heb 12, Luke 13)
Pay attention: God is still speaking wisdom, still revealing truth, and still breathing new life in our world.

Call to Worship (Jer 1, Ps 71)
>Come to Christ, our rock...
>>**our refuge and our strength.**
>Come to listen for God...
>>**our wisdom and our truth.**
>Come to receive the Spirit...
>>**the breath of life itself.**

Opening Prayer (Jer 1, Luke 13)
>Still-speaking God,
>>open our ears to hear your voice;
>>open our minds to perceive your wisdom;
>>and open our eyes to recognize your healing love
>>>and your powerful presence. Amen.

Proclamation and Response

Prayer of Confession (Jer 1, Ps 71, Luke 13)
>Gracious God, you have known us
>>since the beginning of time.
>You know when we struggle to hear your voice,
>>and when we yearn to know your grace.
>Speak to us with wisdom and love,
>>and protect us with mercy and grace.
>Heal us and set us free,
>>that we may recognize your presence,
>>>heed your call,
>>>>and celebrate your loving acceptance.

Words of Assurance (Ps 71, Luke 13)
>Women and men, in the gracious love of Christ,
>>you are set free from your sickness, sin and sorrow.
>Rejoice, for the Rock of Ages has rescued us all.

Introduction to the Word (Jer 1)
> We may or may not know how to listen,
>> but God will speak to us anyway.
> Listen for the word of God.

Response to the Word (Jer 1, Ps 71)
> Where God sends us,
>> **we must go.**
> What God tells us,
>> **we must speak.**
> When God rescues us,
>> **we must rejoice.**
> When God calls us,
>> **we can lean on God, our rock and refuge,**
>> **and need never be afraid.**

Thanksgiving and Communion

Invitation to the Offering (Jer 1, Luke 13)
> Don't think because you're only a child, you don't have gifts to give. Don't think because you're sick and grieving, you don't have healing to offer. Don't think because you're afraid, you don't have courage to share. In Christ, our weaknesses are made strong. Through our offerings, God creates miracles. No matter who you are or where you are on life's journey, your gifts are needed in God's world.

Offering Prayer (Jer 1)
> Holy Spirit, bless these gifts
>> with the power of your love and grace,
>>> that others may recognize your presence
>>> and hear your wisdom and truth.

Sending Forth

Benediction (Jer 1)
As we speak what we have heard,
God will give us the words.
As we go where we are sent,
Christ will lead the way.
As we love as we are loved,
the Spirit will work through our lives.

September 1, 2019

Twelfth Sunday after Pentecost, Proper 17
Karen Clark Ristine

Color

Green

Scripture Readings

Jeremiah 2:4-13; Psalm 81:1, 10-16; Hebrews 13:1-8, 15-16; Luke 14:1, 7-14

Theme Ideas

Jeremiah and Psalm 81 are both laments that God's people do not listen. The scriptures this week remind us to listen for the voice of the Divine and to be attentive to all the ways we find holy sustenance. They call us to rejoice in this awareness. Hebrews and Luke call us to have empathy for others and care for them as we have been cared for by God. Listen. Rejoice. Care. Share God's sustenance with others.

Invitation and Gathering

Centering Words (Ps 81)

"You satisfy the hungry heart with gift of finest wheat. Come give to us, O saving Lord, the bread of life to eat."
—*Omer Westendorf, "You Satisfy the Hungry Heart"*

Call to Worship (Ps 81)
>Sing Aloud.
>Shout for Joy.
>Listen for the voice of God.
>Listen and be fed.
>Listen and be satisfied.
>Sing Aloud.
>Shout for Joy.
>Listen.

Opening Prayer (Ps 81, Heb 13)
>Gracious and sustaining God,
>>we are ready to listen and eager to hear.
>Speak to us through word and song,
>>prayer and silence,
>>>community and communion.
>Offer us the spiritual sustenance
>>that allows us to share with strangers and friends,
>>>that your love may prevail in every encounter.
>Amen.

Proclamation and Response

Prayer of Confession (Jer 2, Ps 81)
>Ever present God, help us in our weakness.
>We do not always listen for your voice.
>We do not always acknowledge the many ways
>>you sustain us in life and faith.
>We feast on your providence,
>>yet wonder if you are near.
>Forgive our past indifference,
>>as we pledge to be more attentive
>>>to your presence and guidance.

Forgive our past selfishness,
as we promise to share the feast of your bounty
with those in need.
For actions and inactions that have hurt your heart
and the well-being of others,
we seek your forgiveness and grace.

Words of Assurance
In the name of Jesus Christ, you are forgiven.
In the name of Jesus Christ, you are forgiven.

Response to the Word (Heb 13, Luke 14)
We will humble ourselves
at the banquet of this holy feast.
We will share all we have and all we are
in the name of Christ.

Thanksgiving and Communion

Offering Prayer (Heb 13, Luke 14)
Receive our gifts, Holy One,
and attune our awareness
to those who are in need.
May today's offering help welcome the stranger,
uphold the prisoner, feed the hungry,
and lift the poor and needy from poverty. Amen.

Great Thanksgiving (Jer 2, Ps 81, Heb 13, Luke 14)
The Lord be with you.
And also with you.
Let us pray.
This is a feast provided by the God
who led our ancestors in faith out of Egypt,

who fed them in the wilderness with manna,
and who quenched their thirst with water from rock.
This feast is sustenance from the same creator
who led God's people safely through a barren land
that no one passes through.
This is a feast from the very God who delivers us
from our own times of deep darkness.
Listen and be fed.
Listen and be satisfied.

This is a feast celebrated by Jesus the Christ
with his disciples—
a feast that is now shared with us.
For Jesus Christ is the same yesterday and today
and forever.
This feast is offered freely to all.
Share this feast with one another.
Share this feast with strangers.
Humble yourself,
and be exalted through this spiritual feast.
Let mutual love continue.

Sending Forth

Benediction (Luke 14)

Go from this place, filled with the spiritual sustenance
of God, your creator.
Go from this place, filled with the feast
Christ shares with all disciples.
Go from this place, led by the Holy Spirit
to share this feast with all. Amen.

September 8, 2019

Thirteenth Sunday after Pentecost, Proper 18
James Dollins

Color

Green

Scripture Readings

Jeremiah 18:1-11; Psalm 139:1-6, 13-18; Philemon 1-21;
Luke 14:25-33

Theme Ideas

The calling that Jesus issues so boldly, even shockingly,
in our Luke passage: "Carry the cross...give up all your
possessions...," "[reject] father, mother, wife and children!" is possible only if the one who calls us also knows
us completely—like the Potter knows the clay (Jeremiah
18), and the Lord knows the fibers of our being (Psalm
139). Similarly, in Philemon, Paul knows Onesimus so
well that he advocates for his liberation from slavery.
Though these passages do not fit neatly together, we
hear overtones of a life-changing calling that is ground-
ed in our belonging to the one who gives us life.

Invitation and Gathering

Centering Words (Jer 18, Ps 139, Luke 14)
Come, be reshaped and recreated
    by the hands of the Potter.
Come, be your true self,
    wonderfully made by God.
Come, that you may hear the Spirit calling.

Call to Worship or Opening Prayer (Ps 139)
O Lord, you have searched me you know me.
    You know when I sit down and when I rise.
    You discern my thoughts from far away.
I praise you, for I am fearfully and wonderfully made.
    Wonderful are your works.
    This I know very well.
With all your children,
    I will give you thanks and praise!

Opening Prayer (Jer 18, Ps 139, Luke 14)
Dear God our creator,
    you have fashioned us carefully with your hands.
We have come to offer you our worship and praise.
You know us better than we know ourselves,
    and you alone comprehend the value
        of every creature and of all that exists.
Help us become all that we were created to be,
    and help us love you and our neighbors
        with all that we are.
May we follow the way of Jesus,
    not in the hope of what we might gain,
        but for all we might give
            in the spirit and joy of Christ,
                in whose name we pray. Amen.

Proclamation and Response

Prayer of Confession (Luke 14)

Spirit of Jesus, walk among us
as you walked with your followers long ago.
Touch us, heal us, and send us to a world
longing for your grace.
Forgive us when we seek your blessings for ourselves,
while hesitating to heed your call to serve others.
Correct us when we dwell on what we lack,
while neglecting to share what we have received.
Free us, Spirit of Christ, to live and to love
as generously as you have loved us.
This we pray in your holy name. Amen.

Words of Assurance (Phlm)

God has forgiven us, freed us,
and called us to serve with joy.
The grace of the Lord Jesus Christ be with you.
Amen.

*Response to the Word (Luke 14, Jer 18, adapted excerpts
from Wesley's Covenant Service)*

Amazingly, God has given God's own self to us
through the life of Jesus Christ.
Let us respond in kind, giving our lives to God
and to the world that God has made:
Lord, let us be your servants,
under your command.
We put ourselves fully into your hands.
Enable our action.
Strengthen our courage.
Let us be employed for you,
or laid aside for you.

Let us be full.
Let us be empty.
Let us have all things.
Let us have nothing.
With free and willing hearts,
we offer ourselves and our gifts
for your pleasure and for your will.

Thanksgiving and Communion

Offering Prayer (Luke 14, Phlm)
Generous God, by your grace
we are free to follow wherever Jesus leads,
and to serve whomever you give us to serve.
May the gifts that we offer here
help comfort those who mourn,
feed those who are hungry,
and liberate those who suffer.
Inspire your church to be united in joyful service
to the beautiful world you have made. Amen.

Sending Forth

Benediction (Luke 14, Jer 18)
May the God whose hands have made us,
whose grace has saved us,
and whose Son walks with us,
lead us forward to share joy with the world,
in the name of the Creator, the Savior,
and the Comforter. Amen.

September 15, 2019

Fourteenth Sunday after Pentecost, Proper 19
Rebecca J. Kruger Gaudino

Color

Green

Scripture Readings

Jeremiah 4:11-12, 22-28; Psalm 14; 1 Timothy 1:12-17; Luke 15:1-10

Theme Ideas

While many of us are uncomfortable speaking about sin today, we all know the pain and remorse we feel when we remember actions that we deeply regret. Paul (if he is the epistle's author) remembers his life as a persecutor. Indeed, if not for his conversion, we would know him only as a collaborator in the execution of Stephen. But Paul testifies to an overwhelming presence that permits him, with the assurance of forgiveness, to live beyond the acts he regrets. Patiently merciful, God sought Paul, like a shepherd looking for a lost sheep and a woman seeking a lost coin. The parables point out the special importance of the lost to God.

Invitation and Gathering

Centering Words (1 Tim 1)

I lay my burdens down, Lord. Take my regrets. Grant me peace.

Call to Worship (1 Tim 1, Luke 15)

Hear the good news:
People who are lost are being found.
Glory, glory; hallelujah!
Hear the good news:
God goes out into the wilderness of *our* lives,
seeking us when *we* are lost.
Glory, glory; hallelujah!
To Christ Jesus, full of faith and love;
to the Ruler of the Ages, immortal, invisible;
to the Spirit of peace and mercy,
all honor and glory are yours
forever and ever. Amen!

Opening Prayer (1 Tim 1, Luke 15)

Christ Jesus, we stand in your presence,
remembering your amazing welcome
of all who are lost and fallen.
Sometimes we feel as if we too belong in this group,
for we've fallen short of who we might be.
Still, we come into your presence
with confidence in your love;
and we praise you for the acceptance
that you show us all.
To you be honor and glory, forever and ever. Amen.

Proclamation and Response

Prayer of Confession (Jer 4, 1 Tim 1)
> Gracious and loving God,
>> we find it difficult at times
>>> to place our trust in you.
>
> Too often we look at the world,
>> and see only violence, pain, destruction,
>>> and signs of hopelessness and despair.
>
> Too often we rely on our own strength,
>> our own plans, our own devices,
>>> rather than trusting in your hand to hold us,
>>>> your love to sustain us,
>>>>> and your wisdom to see us through.
>
> Forgive us, Holy One.
> Help us turn to you when we are lost,
>> that we might find our way home.
>
> Help us navigate the treacherous waters of this world,
>> that we might experience your abundant grace,
>>> mercy, and love.
>
> Help us put our trust in you,
>> that the faith and love that are in Christ Jesus
>>> may shine in our lives for all to see. Amen.
>
> *(Karin Ellis)*

Words of Assurance (Luke 15:7 NRSV)
> Jesus said, "there will be more joy in heaven
>> over one sinner who repents than over ninety-nine
>> righteous persons who need no repentance."
>
> My friends, experience God's forgiveness and joy—
>> gifts that leads to new life!
>
> *(Karin Ellis)*

Passing the Peace of Christ (Luke 15)

Jesus welcomed all who came into his presence. So let us welcome one another with the peace of Christ.

Prayer of Preparation (1 Tim 1)

You are the Living Word, Christ Jesus,
who strengthens us and calls us to faithful service.
May we hear you today
in the reading of your word. Amen.
(Perhaps children could act out the parts of the parables with appropriate props: stuffed toy lamb, a broom, and large silver coin.)

Response to the Word (1 Tim 1, Luke 15)

Our Savior Jesus seeks us
in the wilderness of our own lives.
Jesus is more than all our regrets.
So today, here, let us lay down any burdens
that we are weary of bearing.
Free in Christ, may we walk with our spirits lightened,
through the love of Jesus.
What might you want to lay down today?
(moment of silence)
Forgive us where we have done wrong,
and lift our sorrow and pain from us.
Help us live beyond our regrets,
for you are the one who forgives us,
and who gives us a fresh start. Amen.

Thanksgiving and Communion

Invitation to the Offering (1 Tim 1, Luke 15)

Let us share the love we receive from God with others,
through the gifts we give this morning.

Offering Prayer (1 Tim 1, Luke 15)
Loving God, your Son came into this world
    to save us all with overflowing grace,
        and faithful love.
Bless all the offerings we bring today,
    that these gifts might demonstrate your welcome
        to all who are fallen.
Bring the lost home, dear Jesus.
Bring them home in peace. Amen.

Sending Forth

Benediction (1 Tim 1, Luke 15)
Go forth like a shepherd:
    Seek the lost.
    Seek the fallen.
    Welcome the sinner.
    Bring them home.
Always remember that our eternal dwelling
    is the very presence of God.
Rejoice, for our God has found us
    and carries us home.
    To Christ Jesus, our Lord,
        who loves us and will not let us go:
        Glory, glory! Hallelujah!

September 22, 2019

Fifteenth Sunday after Pentecost, Proper 20
B. J. Beu
[Copyright © B. J. Beu. Used by permission.]

Color

Green

Scripture Readings

Jeremiah 8:18–9:1; Psalm 79:1-9; 1 Timothy 2:1-7; Luke 16:1-13

Theme Ideas

Stewardship is a natural way to focus these readings. While Jeremiah and the psalmist cry out to God for help in the midst of Israel's distress, there is much that faith communities can do to ease the suffering of others. In Luke, Jesus tells a perplexing parable about the dishonest steward who, after being fired for mismanaging his master's accounts, acts shrewdly to ingratiate himself to those who owe his master money. Jesus challenges the children of light to be as wise with their generation as this dishonest steward. Proper management of our time, talents, and treasure matters, for if we cannot be trusted to be good stewards of dishonest wealth, how can God trust us to be faithful stewards of true riches?

Invitation and Gathering

Centering Words (Luke 16)

Whoever is faithful in a very little is also faithful in much; and whoever is unfaithful with a very little is also unfaithful in much. May we, who are asked to give an accounting of our lives, be found faithful.

Call to Worship (Jer 8, Ps 79)

Cry out to the Lord, for God hears our pleas.
**May our heads be springs of water
and our eyes fountains of tears,
for God answers the cries of the suffering.**
Put your faith in God, our great physician.
**We will reach out for the balm of Gilead,
for God soothes the sorrows of the faithful.**
Call upon the Lord,
for God hears our pleas.
**We will enter God's gates
with hope and gladness.**
Come, worship the one who hears our pleas.

Opening Prayer (Jer 8:22, Ps 79)

Righteous and ever-faithful God,
speed your compassion to our side,
for we are brought low in our need.
We come to you in this time of worship,
for our spirits are poured out like water,
and there is no one to heal our pain.
Do not remain unmoved when the scoffers say:
"Is there no balm in Gilead?
Is there no physician there?"
Help us, O God of our salvation,

and come speedily to us once more,
  that all may see your glory
    and know where our true help lies. Amen.

Proclamation and Response

Prayer of Confession or Prayer of Yearning (Ps 79, 1 Tim 2, Luke 16)

Holy One, your ways are as far above our ways
  as the heavens are above the raging seas.
We yearn to offer supplications, prayers, intercessions,
  and thanksgiving for the needs of all,
    but find some people hard to love.
We long to be faithful stewards of your many blessings,
  but often find the effort a hassle
    in the midst of more pleasurable pursuits.
Forgive us when we try to serve two masters—
  when we seek the shelter and safety of your love,
    while placing our trust in human wealth,
      status, and power.
Heal our brokenness and our self-centered ways,
  for you alone are our one true physician,
    and you alone can make us well. Amen.

Assurance of Pardon (Jer 8, 1 Tim 2)

The author of our salvation,
  the one who weeps for us and for our world,
    is the God of compassion.
God meets us in our need
  and heals our many failing.
Rejoice and be glad.

Passing the Peace of Christ (1 Tim 2)

When we offer supplications, prayers, intercessions, and thanksgiving for others, we discover a peace that passes all understanding. Let us share signs of this peace as we pass the peace of Christ.

Response to the Word (1 Tim 2)

Take heart, sisters and brothers in Christ,
  God desires that everyone be saved.
Rest in this truth and put your faith in Christ,
  our mediator between heaven and earth,
  the one who saves us in holy love.

Thanksgiving and Communion

Offering Prayer (Luke 16)

God of manifold blessings,
  you provide for our every need,
    and call us to be good stewards
      of your many gifts.
May we be found faithful in a little,
  that we may also be faithful in a lot.
We offer you these gifts in loving gratitude,
  that they may shine forth in the world
    and bring your children everywhere
      your healing love and light.
In Jesus' name, we pray. Amen.

Sending Forth

Benediction (Luke 16)

Go forth and be faithful in a little,
  that you may also be found faithful in much.

Go to be faithful in much,
     that you may be entrusted
     with the wealth and welfare of others.
Go to be faithful with the wealth of this generation,
     that you may be given the true riches
     that come from above.
Go to be faithful children of light,
     that you may know the grace, hope, and peace
     of the one who is truly faithful.

September 29, 2019

Sixteenth Sunday after Pentecost, Proper 21
Karin Ellis

Color

Green

Scripture Readings

Jeremiah 32:1-3a, 6-15; Psalm 91:1-6, 14-16; 1 Timothy
6:6-19; Luke 16:19-31

Theme Ideas

The scriptures for today remind us to live in God's ways,
even when life is pulling us away from God. The prophet Jeremiah speaks to the Israelites who have been held
captive in Babylon. Though they are in a foreign land,
living under a different ruler, in a different culture, and
trying to hold onto their religion, Jeremiah proclaims
that, even in this situation, there is hope. The ability to
purchase land and settle down, even in a foreign land,
is a sign of hope of God's providence. The psalmist uses
the image of God as refuge and fortress—someone to
turn to when the world around us is swirling in darkness and distress. We cling to God's love because we
are God's people. First Timothy reminds us that we are

called to follow Christ and not allow worldly things to overwhelm us or to guide our lives. Our true guide is Christ, the "King of kings and Lord of lords." And the Gospel of Luke points to the way of a godly life. We are to follow God's ways and build a strong relationship with God through Jesus Christ, each and every day of our lives.

Invitation and Gathering

Centering Words (1 Tim 6)
In this moment, in this space, focus on God. May faith take hold of us so completely that we begin to live as Christ calls us to live.

Call to Worship (Ps 91, Luke 16)
When we are lost and uncertain,
God provides prophets and storytellers
to guide us toward the truth.
When we are in need of rescue,
God provides refuge and shelter
during our darkest days.
When we are looking, seeking, and hoping,
God provides open arms to welcome us
with love and faithfulness.
Come! Let us worship.

Opening Prayer (Jer 32, 1 Tim 6, Luke 16)
Loving God, our rock and foundation,
we thank you for the opportunity
to gather in your holy name.
May this be a time when we remember
your faithfulness.

You give us hope
    when despair creeps into our lives.
You carve out a path
    when we lack direction.
You send family members, friends, and even strangers
    when we need reminders of your promise.
And you send Jesus Christ, your beloved Son,
    to show us how to live in your ways.
May we open our hearts
    to receive all that you provide. Amen.

Proclamation and Response

Prayer of Confession (Jer 32, Luke 16)
God, you are the stronghold of our lives.
When life takes us to places we never imagined,
    you provide hope and bring us back to you.
Forgive the times when we abandon your ways.
Forgive our failure to see your presence in our lives.
Forgive us when we hurt ourselves and one another.
Forgive our fear of those who are different.
Forgive our failure to care for one another.
Gracious God, forgive us and heal us.
Help us return to your open and loving arms,
    trusting you as the Lord of our lives.
In Christ's name, we pray. Amen.

Words of Assurance (Ps 91)
The psalmist proclaims, "My refuge and my fortress;
    my God in whom I trust."
May we trust the forgiveness of God
    that sets us free and enables us
    to joyfully be the people of God.

In the name of Christ, you are forgiven.
In the name of Christ, you are forgiven.
Amen.

Passing the Peace of Christ (1 Tim 6)

The light of Christ is upon us. Turn and greet one another with the peace of Christ, allowing Christ's light to shine among us.

Prayer of Preparation (Luke 16)

God of us all, open our ears,
    that we may hear the stories
        told by our ancestors.
Open our hearts,
    that we may understand the movement
        of your Spirit in our lives.
Open our hands,
    that we may serve you
        and care for one another. Amen.

Response to the Word (1 Tim 6)

May the words we have heard spoken
    take root in our lives,
    that we "may take hold of the life
        that really is life"—
        a life led by Christ and nourished by God's
        amazing love.

Thanksgiving and Communion

Invitation to the Offering (1 Tim 6, Luke 16)

We are not asked to hold fast to our treasures; rather,
God invites us to share what we have, so that the king-

dom of God may flourish. In thanksgiving and praise for God's abundance, let us offer what we can for the glory of God.

Offering Prayer (Jer 32)

Generous and almighty God,
>we offer these gifts to you.

We are thankful for your providence,
>but we are even more grateful
>>that we can share these gifts with you
>>>and with your children everywhere.

May these gifts be signs of our faithfulness to you
>and to one another.

In your holy name, we pray. Amen.

Sending Forth

Benediction (1 Tim 6, Luke 16)

Brothers and sisters, go to live with God
>every moment of each day.

May the love of God, the peace of Christ,
>and the guidance of the Holy Spirit,
>help us to build strong, faithful, relationships.

Go in peace. Amen.

October 6, 2019

World Communion Sunday, Proper 22
Hans Holznagel

Color

Green or White

Scripture Readings

Lamentations 1:1-6; Psalm 137; 2 Timothy 1:1-14; Luke 17:5-10

Theme Ideas

World Communion Sunday often focuses on unity at God's table, a vision of the beloved community. In a different tone, today's texts invite an unblinking look at the calamities and upheavals affecting brothers and sisters nearby and far away: war, conquest, displacement, economic crisis, grinding poverty, even natural disaster. Faith calls us to see and testify that these exist and that their causes are often human. To lament and to grieve with the afflicted can prompt the spirit of courage to act, even if only with a mustard seed of faith.

Invitation and Gathering

Centering Words (2 Tim 1)

Do not be ashamed to testify in faith and love. God gives
us not a spirit of cowardice, but of power and love.

Call to Worship (Ps 137, Lam 1, Luke 17, 2 Tim 1)

Sometimes life is torn down, war does not cease,
home is far away.
Affliction comes. People weep. Suffering prevails.
So it is, in many places near and far.
**But it need not be the end. Let lament
and compassion activate our faith this day.**

Opening Prayer (Lam 1, 2 Tim 1)

On this World Communion Sunday,
   we thank you, O God, for the reminder
     that we are not alone.
In every age people have known joy and struggle.
So it is in this moment.
Grant us wisdom, courage and discipline,
   that we might see and testify to this truth.
May we weep with those who weep,
   even as we ourselves have been comforted.
We pray in the spirit of grace, mercy and peace. Amen.

Proclamation and Response

Prayer of Confession (Ps 137, Lam 1, Luke 17)

We confess our compassion to you, creator God,
   and ask only that you increase it.
Let our intimate knowledge of weeping
   expand into concern and caring for a world

so often wracked with tragedy.
Let us not worry that we have to fix it all.
Let us rather be encouraged, in compassion,
    to do the things we know we ought to do.
In Jesus' name, we pray. Amen.

Words of Assurance (2 Tim 1, Luke 17)
Know that sincere faith—
    even faith the size of a tiny seed—
        can work wonders in all of us.
Embrace the compassion and the promise of life
    that is in Christ Jesus. Amen.

Response to the Word (2 Tim 1)
Let gifts of grace, mercy, and peace
    be rekindled within us,
        relying on the power of God.

Thanksgiving and Communion

Offering Prayer (Ps 137, Lam 1)
Mindful of people whose worlds are falling apart,
    we offer these gifts and our very lives
        for the repair of worlds, near and far,
            that need your care—
                in ways large and small. Amen.

Invitation to Communion (Ps 137, Lam 1)
As we dwell in the beauty of our unity at table
    with our sisters and brothers around the world,
    it is good to remember our brokenness.

War, displacement, exile, economic crisis,
    natural disaster: all have been known
    for thousands of years, as they are today.
At the table, we accompany the afflicted
    and seek comfort and renewal for ourselves,
    that we may be agents of the same
    to a world in need.
All are welcome here.

Sending Forth

Benediction (Ps 137, Lam 1, Luke 17, 2 Tim 1)
    Do not be ashamed to testify to the truth.
    Join the afflicted in lament and grief.
    Guard the good treasure entrusted to you:
        a seed of faith, a spirit of courage.
    Go forth in peace. Amen.

October 13, 2019

Eighteenth Sunday after Pentecost, Proper 23
Mary Scifres
[Copyright © Mary Scifres. Used by permission.]

Color

Green

Scripture Readings

Jeremiah 29:1, 4-7; Psalm 66:1-12; 2 Timothy 2:8-15; Luke 17:11-19

Theme Ideas

Finding hope in hopeless situations challenges us on our journeys of life and faith, but today's scriptures lift examples of people who did just that. Jeremiah calls the Israelites to thrive, even in exile, and to create the beauty and wholeness of shalom (welfare) right where they've been exiled. Endurance and steadfast faithfulness, even in the midst of imprisonment and persecution, are themes of today's passage from 2 Timothy. Perhaps most poignantly of all, ten outcasts with leprosy are welcomed into health and wholeness when they cry out to Jesus for mercy, even though only one of them returns to give thanks. Hope binds us to God's promises, just as hope binds these four disparate scriptures together thematically.

Invitation and Gathering

Centering Words (Jer 29, Luke 17)

Hope in the midst of hopelessness can create miracles, even in the worst of times.

Call to Worship (Jer 29, Ps 66, Luke 17)

Sing and shout with joy,

for the God of hope is with us now.

Give thanks and praise to God,

for the God of hope is with us always.

Come and see God's deeds,

and discover the miraculous power

of unending hope.

Opening Prayer (Jer 29, 2 Tim 2)

God of all hopefulness,

bring hope to our weary world

and to our troubled hearts;

ignite hope within our worship this day.

Strengthen our faith as children of hope,

that we may to partner with you

and share the good news

of your steadfast faithfulness with the world.

Proclamation and Response

Prayer of Confession (Jer 29, 2 Tim 2, Luke 17)

Reassure us, faithful God,

when doubt troubles our thoughts.

Comfort us in times of despair.

Forgive us in moments of sin.

Heal us in seasons of sickness and sorrow.
Have mercy on us, O God,
> that we may have mercy on your beautiful world,
> > creating shalom in all that we say and do.
In the spirit of your hope and love, we pray. Amen.

Words of Assurance (Ps 66, Luke 17)

Shout and sing for joy!
Christ has brought us out to freedom,
> and our faith has healed us and made us whole.

Passing the Peace of Christ (Jer 29)

Pray for the peace of the places you are sent, the people with whom you dwell, and the world in which you reside. In this spirit of shalom, let us share signs of peace and love.

Introduction to the Word (2 Tim 2)

Rather than engaging in battles over what these scriptures means or arguing over understandings that evolve over time, let's open our hearts and minds to whatever new inspiration God is offering us this day.

Response to the Word (Jer 29, Luke 17)

Like the Israelites in exile,
may we bring gifts in hard places:
> **hope to a hurting world;**
beauty to brighten our days;
> **peace in the midst of strife;**
shalom where people are broken;
> **life and growth where death has threatened.**
Like Jesus on the way to the cross,
> **may we offer healing love to one and all.**

Thanksgiving and Communion

Invitation to the Offering (Jer 29, Luke 17)

Bring your gratitude, bring your gifts, bring your
prayers, bring your blessings. May our offerings be living prayers for the welfare of the world.

Offering Prayer (Jer 29, 2 Tim 2, Luke 17)

For bringing hope to our world and healing to our lives,
we give you thanks and praise.
Bless these gifts,
that they may become signs of hope,
paths of healing,
and prayers of peace for your world.

Sending Forth

Benediction (Jer 29, Luke 17)

With the hope of all hopefulness,
the steadfast faith of the hopeful,
and the faithful assurance of the healed,
go now to bring hope and healing
to the world.

October 20, 2019

Nineteenth Sunday after Pentecost, Proper 24
B. J. Beu
[Copyright © B. J. Beu. Used by permission.]

Color
Green

Scripture Readings
Jeremiah 31:27-34; Psalm 119:97-104; 2 Timothy 3:14–4:5; Luke 18:1-8

Theme Ideas
The inspiration of scripture, the value of holding fast to God's teachings, the need to keep the faith, and God's promise to put a new covenant in our hearts tie these scriptures together. Jeremiah, the psalmist, and Paul all attest to the value of following and meditating upon God's teachings. Luke adds Jesus' admonition to constantly bring our petitions before God, who will hear and hearken to our pleas for justice.

Invitation and Gathering

Centering Words (Luke 16)
Taste and see that the Lord is good.
God's blessings are sweeter than honey.

Call to Worship (Ps 119)

Taste and see that the Lord is good.
God's blessings are sweeter than honey.
God keeps our feet from wandering down wrong paths.
God's precepts make us wiser
than those who are accounted wise.
Let us worship the one who guides our lives.
Let us worship the one who leads us into life.

Opening Prayer (Ps 119, 2 Tim 3–4)

God of discernment and truth,
be with us in our time of worship.
Open our minds to receive your wisdom.
Open our hearts to accept your love.
Open our spirits to embrace your ways.
Be present with us as we seek your guidance,
that we may follow in your wisdom and truth.
Amen.

Proclamation and Response

Prayer of Confession or Prayer of Yearning (Jer 31)

Everlasting God, we need your hand to guide us.
You watch over us
and help us chart the seasons of our lives.
Instruct us when it is time to pluck up
and when it is time to break down.
Teach us when it is time to build
and when it is time to tear down.
Show us when it is time to sow
and when it is time to reap.
Make a new covenant with us
and put your teachings in our hearts.

Be our God,
  that we may be your people—
    a people who know you
      and who keep your ways. Amen.

Words of Assurance (Jer 31)
  In the new covenant of Christ Jesus,
    grace and forgiveness are ours.
  Rejoice and live into the hope and freedom
    that are ours.

Passing the Peace of Christ (Ps 119)
  Words of peace are sweeter than honey. Taste and see
  that the Lord is good as you pass the peace of Christ
  with one another.

Invitation to the Word (2 Tim 3)
  The word of God is useful for teaching,
    for correction, and for training in righteousness,
    that everyone who belongs to God may be proficient
    and equipped for every good work.
  Listen for the word of God.

Response to the Word (Ps 119, 2 Tim 3)
  O God, we love to study your word.
    When we are lost,
    your teachings guide and save us.
  When others seek to lead us astray,
  your word leads us into truth.
    Like the sweet taste of honey
    are your words to our lips.
  Sweeter than candy
  are your teachings in our mouth.

Your sacred word saves us,
through faith in Christ Jesus.
O God, how we love to study your word.

Thanksgiving and Communion

Offering Prayer (Jer 31, Ps 119)
    God of abundant blessing,
        may our gifts become instruments of your truth
            and vessels of your love;
        may our offerings plant seeds of hope
            wherever they are planted;
        may these gifts build a world of justice
            and righteousness for all.
    In Christ's name, we pray. Amen.

Sending Forth

Benediction (2 Tim 3–4)
    Continue in what you have learned and firmly believed,
        and hold fast to the sacred writings
            that are able to instruct you in the ways of salvation
            through faith in Christ Jesus.
    Go forth to proclaim the message you have heard.
    Go forth to be the people of God.

October 27, 2019

Twentieth Sunday after Pentecost, Reformation Sunday, Proper 25
Mary Scifres
[Copyright © Mary Scifres. Used by permission.]

Color

Green

Scripture Readings

Joel 2:23-32; Psalm 65; 2 Timothy 4:6-8, 16-18; Luke 18:9-14

Theme Ideas

The tension between humility and righteous faithfulness finds voice in the New Testament lections today: Jesus condemning the Pharisee for pride and self-righteousness, whereas the letter-writer of 2 Timothy lauds the author's faithful righteousness as a testament to God's protection and providential power. The proclamation of God's protection for this righteous leader seems in direct contrast to the lesson lifted in Luke 18:9-14. But isn't this tension the truth of scripture? After all, Joel's prophecy of abundant blessings and spiritual strength is offered to a people who are feeling bereft and powerless. The tension of the now and the not yet, the humble and the proud, the confident and the doubtful offers the worship leader an opportunity to honor the rich and paradoxical lessons within scripture.

Invitation and Gathering

Centering Words (Joel 2, 2 Tim 4, Luke 18)
Living in this world, while yearning for a better, has long been our story as the children of God. Prayers for blessings find voice amidst cries of lament, and words of confidence are spoken in moments of doubt. Run the race and move forward in faith, trusting that God will lift us up even when we are at the lowest points of our lives.

Call to Worship (Joel 2, Luke 18)
The Spirit is here,
>**bringing vision and hope for our world.**

Christ lifts us up,
>**welcoming us with loving arms.**

God showers the earth,
>**nourishing all creation with grace.**

Sense the Spirit moving within and among us.
>**Feel Christ's presence healing and blessing us.**

As we gather in worship this day,
>**we receive the showering love of God.**

Opening Prayer (Joel 2, 2 Tim 4)
God of Zion, strengthen us for the journey ahead.
Lift our eyes to the hills,
>that we may see the light
>>of your gracious loving presence.

Open our minds to your visions and dreams,

that we may claim our place
as your children,
and we may run with faithfulness
the race set before us.
In your holy name, we pray. Amen.

Proclamation and Response

Prayer of Confession or Prayer of Yearning (Joel 2, 2 Tim 4, Luke 18)
Gracious God, have mercy on us
in our times of sin and pride.
Pour out your forgiveness,
and shower us with the blessings
of your guidance and grace.
Stand by us in our times of weakness,
and strengthen us to move forward in faith.
Help us finish this race with gratitude and joy,
that others may receive the blessings
of all you are doing through us
and all you have yet to do.

Words of Assurance (2 Tim 4)
God will rescue us from every evil action,
even as Christ is saving us
for God's heavenly realm.

—Or—

Words of Assurance (Luke 18)
You, who have been brought low,
are lifted and brought high
in the saving grace of Christ,
the mighty love of God.

Response to the Word or Benediction (2 Tim 4)
Keep the faith,
even when doubt is all around.
Fight the fight,
when justice and love seem far away.
Run the race with confidence,
for Christ is leading the way.

Thanksgiving and Communion

Invitation to the Offering (Joel 2, 2 Tim 4, Luke 18)
Bring your dreams, bring your visions, bring your
prayers, bring your presence, bring your gifts, and bring
your witness. All of these offerings are blessings to God.

Offering Prayer (Joel 2, 2 Tim 4, Luke 18)
For refreshing autumn rain
and for sparkling dew in the morning,
we thank you, generous God.
For humbling lessons
and for prophetic calls to discipleship,
we thank you, challenging God.
For reassuring words of comfort
and for your powerfully protective love,
we thank you, gracious God.
In thanksgiving and gratitude,
we return a portion of these gifts to you
and ask that you transform these gifts
into blessings for a world in need.

Sending Forth

Benediction (Joel 2, 2 Tim 4, Luke 18)
Go forth with confidence as the followers of God.
Go forth with humility as sisters and brothers of Christ.
And abide in courage
as visionary sons and daughters of the Holy Spirit.

November 3, 2019

Twenty-first Sunday after Pentecost, Proper 26
B. J. Beu
[Copyright © B. J. Beu. Used by permission.]

Color

Green

Scripture Readings

Habakkuk 1:1-4; 2:1-4; Psalm 119:137-44; 2 Thessalonians 1:1-4, 11-12; Luke 19:1-10

Theme Ideas

Watching and waiting is central to the spiritual life. In the face of injustice and abuse by the powerful, Habakkuk declares that he will watch and wait until God answers his petition for justice. In response to Habakkuk's vigil, God promises a vision that does not lie—a vision where the righteous shall live by faith. Zacchaeus climbs a tree as he waits to see Jesus. In response, salvation comes to his house that day. The psalmist proclaims God's righteousness and delight in God's precepts. Surely this righteousness came to pass while a person of faith watched and waited in prayerful expectation. Can we do less?

Invitation and Gathering

Centering Words (Hab 2)

Stand at your watchpost and watch for a vision.
If it seems to tarry, wait for it.
It will surely come.
It will not delay.

Call to Worship (Hab 1, 2)

Stand at your watchpost and wait for the Lord.
We wait for a vision of truth and hope.
Stand at your watchpost and pray to the Lord.
We pray for justice and righteousness.
Stand at your watchpost and trust in the Lord.
We trust the one who hears our cries
and vindicates the pure of heart.
Stand at your watchpost and worship the Lord.

Opening Prayer (Hab 2, Ps 119, Luke 19)

God of righteousness, hear our prayer.
We come before you with zeal in our hearts
  seeking justice for the wronged,
    hope for the downhearted,
      and healing for the afflicted.
We strain to see your face
  and to behold the glory of our salvation.
Visit us with visions of your kingdom
  and transform us in your image,
    that salvation may visit our houses this day.
Amen.

Proclamation and Response

Prayer of Confession or Prayer of Yearning (Hab 1, Luke 19)
God of new beginnings,
>come to us in our need,
>>for we are weary and afraid;
>hear our pleas for mercy,
>>for we are tired and beat down;
>respond to our longing for friendship,
>>for we are despondent and losing hope.
Giver of visions and bestower of every blessing,
>we yearn to know the hope
>>to which we are called.
Heal us with your mercy and compassion,
>that our faith may be rekindled
>>and your salvation may visit our homes this day.

Words of Assurance (Luke 19)
Christ came to save the least and the lost,
>the hopeful and the expectant,
>and all who long for fullness of life.
Today, salvation has come to this house of worship,
>for in Christ, we are God's beloved children,
>forgiven and made whole,
>through the power of the Holy Spirit.

Passing the Peace (Hab 2)
As we stand at our watchposts and wait for a vision, we find others standing and waiting with us. Let us share signs of solidarity and encouragement with one another as we pass the peace of Christ with those who wait for the Lord.

Response to the Word (2 Thess 1)
With overflowing mercy and abundant grace,
God's word blesses us and makes us worthy of our call.
With prayers of hope and songs of joy,
God's word forges us as people of faith
and as children of promise.
With acts of compassion and works of generosity,
share God's word as people of peace.
With lives of love and our souls on fire,
we will plant fruit of the Spirit
wherever we go.

Thanksgiving and Communion

Offering Prayer (Ps 119, Luke 19)
God of many blessings,
as Zacchaeus before us,
we long to see your face
and know the power of your presence.
In moments of sharing and generosity,
we see visions of how our lives and world
are healed and made whole.
Work within these offerings and in our very lives,
that the world may know your hope
and your love. Amen.

Sending Forth

Benediction (Hab 1, 2)
Though the night seems long,
watch and wait for the Lord.
We go to stand at our watchpost.

Though hatred and violence
seem to wield the upper hand.
    We go to see the vision of our salvation.
Though the wicked surround the righteous,
and justice seems perverted.
    We go to proclaim the vindication of our God.
Take heart, people of God,
for God goes with us.
    We go in the peace of Christ
    and the power of the Holy Spirit.

November 10, 2019

Twenty-second Sunday after Pentecost, Proper 27

Mary Scifres

Color

Green

Scripture Readings

Haggai 1:15b–2:9; Psalm 145:1-5, 17-21; 2 Thessalonians 2:1-5, 13-17; Luke 20:27-38

Theme Ideas

Where we focus our thoughts and energies defines our perspective and either opens or limits our possibilities. The Sadducees focus on denying the resurrection and tricking Jesus with challenging questions, and so they experience conflict rather than the new life and learning this holy man brings to their midst. In contrast, Haggai focuses on hope and courage, inviting the Israelites to envision new beginnings and the glorious splendor of living once again as God's chosen people. The writers of Psalm 145 and of 2 Thessalonians focus on gratitude, even in the midst of changing situations, cries of distress, and unknown futures. Focused on thanksgiving, these writers sing praise, proclaim hopeful confidence, and call us to do likewise.

Invitation and Gathering

Centering Words (2 Thess 2, Luke 20)
Focused on Christ, our center, we find faith, hope, life, and love. Anticipating these gifts, we bring our hearts of praise to worship.

Call to Worship (Luke 20)
Children of the living God,
why have you come to this house of worship?
We come to worship the God of the living.
Children of the loving God,
what do you bring to honor the Holy One?
We bring our hearts of hope and love.
Children of the faithful God,
how will you worship our God on high?
We will worship in trust and faith this day.

Opening Prayer (Luke 20, Hag 1)
Living, loving God, breathe among us this day.
Breathe new life into our midst,
that we may remember and reclaim our place
as children of the resurrection.
As we sing our praises and offer our prayers,
speak courage and hope to us,
that our voices may grow in confidence
and our hearts may grow in faith.
In your living presence,
we offer our prayers and praise. Amen.

Proclamation and Response

Prayer of Confession (Hag 1, 2 Thess 2, Luke 20)
When sin floods our lives with deadly temptation,
    lift us from the flood
        into the safety of your mercy and grace.
When our despair overwhelms your vision in our lives,
    shine the truth of hope,
        that your vision may become clear to us
        once more.
When our faith is shaken,
    reclaim us with your steadfast faithfulness.
When death seems ever near,
    speak life to our weary souls.
Restore our focus on Christ our center,
    and revive our purpose and passion
        as we walk joyously with you
        on the path of love and life.

Words of Assurance (Hag 1, 2 Thess 2, Luke 20)
Do not be alarmed in times of trial, temptation,
    and doubt.
Stand firm, for God is with you.
Take courage, for Christ is our strength.
And rest assured, that we are safe in the arms
    of God's love and grace.
In Christ's resurrection, we are given new life
    to be children of the living God,
    now and forevermore.

Passing the Peace of Christ (Hag 1)
The spirit of peace and love abides in each of us. Let us
share this spirit of peace and love with one another.

Introduction to the Word (Luke 20)

Listen for the living word in the words of scripture this day.

Response to the Word (Hag 1, Ps 145, Luke 20)

Great are you, God of life and resurrection,
    for bringing life out of death
        and hope out of despair.
Thank you for awakening us to new life this day,
    as you do each morning when we awaken.
Focus our hearts and minds on this gift of life
    with each breath we take.
Focus our visions and dreams on the hope and promise
    of your constant presence.
Focus our time and talents in service
    and love for your world.
With joyous gratitude, we pray. Amen.

Thanksgiving and Communion

Offering Prayer (Ps 145, Luke 20)

Every day, we bless you and thank you for your gifts.
Today, we return a portion of those gifts to you,
    asking that you bless them.
Through your great mercy,
    may they become life and blessing
        for those in need of your life-giving presence.
Amen.

Sending Forth

Benediction (Ps 145, Luke 20)
As children of the living God,
we go forth with the promise of new life,
the hope of resurrection in our world,
and the passion to keep our hearts
focused on your love and life.

November 17, 2019

Twenty-third Sunday after Pentecost, Proper 28
B. J. Beu
[Copyright © B. J. Beu. Used by permission.]

Color

Green

Scripture Readings

Isaiah 65:17-25; Isaiah 12; 2 Thessalonians 3:6-13; Luke 21:5-19

Theme Ideas

Isaiah proclaims that God is about to create a new heaven and a new earth—the peaceable kingdom where the wolf and the lamb will feed together and everyone will have enough to eat. The psalmist urges us to shout for joy at our salvation. In contrast, Paul chastises the Christians in Thessalonica to get off their duffs and work for their bread. And Jesus proclaims that war and martyrdom are coming, along with famine and plague. New life may be at hand...yet death is ever near. God's people may be blessed with plenty and live to a ripe old age...or the faithful may die at the hands of the unrighteous in the midst of famine and plague. As

Dickens said: "It was the best of times, it was the worst of times." We live our lives between the poles of hope and despair, between visions of what can be and what may be if it all goes horribly wrong. Through it all, we are called to be faithful, for we are given this promise: "By your endurance you will gain your souls" (Luke 21:18-19 NRSV).

Invitation and Gathering

Centering Words (2 Thess 3)

Do not be weary in doing what is right, for by your endurance you will gain your souls.

Call to Worship (Isa 65, Isa 12)

Rejoice and be glad, people of God.
God is making all things new.
Sing for joy, sisters and brothers in Christ.
God bathes us in the well of salvation.
Dance with delight, heirs of the Spirit.
God has turned our sorrow into laughter.
Rejoice and be glad, people of God.
God is making all things new.

—Or—

Call to Worship (Isa 65, Isa 12, Luke 21)

Sing praises to God, sing praises.
Worship God with shouts of joy.
Worship God with songs of gladness.
Worship God with hope and love.
Sing praises to God, sing praises.
Worship God in spirit and in truth.

Opening Prayer (Isa 65, Isa 12, Luke 21)
God of hope and promise,
speak again your words of life and death,
for reports of violence and bloodshed
are all around us.
In a world where refugees have nowhere to turn, bless
us anew with visions of heavenly shalom,
that the world may be healed and your people
may live in safety and peace.
Teach us the joy of sharing simple acts of kindness
and heartfelt gifts of tender mercy,
that we may be people of your kingdom
and children of your love. Amen.

Proclamation and Response

Prayer of Confession or Prayer of Yearning (Isa 65, Isa 12)
Eternal God, your anger may last for a moment,
but your mercy endures for a lifetime.
We come before you with joyful hearts,
longing to draw living water
from the well of your salvation.
We come this day to worship with thankful spirits,
yearning to abide in the new earth
you are creating in our midst.
As we sing your praises,
touch us with the love of your new heaven,
that we may be fit to dwell
in your peaceable kingdom. Amen.

Words of Assurance (Isa 12, Luke 21)
Through Christ, the wellspring of our salvation,
we are washed in the waters of forgiveness

and grace.
Through your endurance, you will gain your souls.

Passing the Peace of Christ *(Isa 65:25 NRSV)*

"The wolf and the lamb shall feed together, / the lion shall eat straw like the ox.... / They shall not hurt or destroy / on all my holy mountain, / says the LORD." The one who is making all things new calls us to lives of peace and harmony. Turn and greet one another in the spirit of reconciliation and unity as we pass the peace of Christ.

Response to the Word *(Isa 65, Luke 21)*

Your new heaven and new earth beckons, O God.
Call us into your future with hope and expectation,
    that in the midst of war, famine and want,
        we may be instruments of your grace
            in your realm without end. Amen.

Thanksgiving and Communion

Offering Prayer *(Isa 65)*

God of visions and dreams,
    as we seek to make a difference in our world,
        teach us anew that your love
            makes all things possible.
Work within our offerings this day,
    that they may be signs of our commitment
        to dream your Dreams
            and to bring your Vision for our world to life.
Work within these gifts,
    that those who have lost hope for a better future
        may find all they need
            to live with passion and purpose. Amen.

Sending Forth

Benediction (Isa 65, 2 Thess 3, Luke 21)
People of God, as you leave this place,
do not grow weary in doing what is right.
We will bring hope and love to all we meet,
and proclaim justice and peace wherever we go.
Sisters and brothers in Christ, as you go forth,
share God's vision of the peaceable kingdom.
We will share God's vision of peace
and work for to bring God's kingdom near.
Children of the Holy Spirit, as you return home,
live this vision and dream into reality.

November 24, 2019

Reign of Christ/Christ the King Sunday, Proper 29

James Dollins

Color

White

Scripture Readings

Jeremiah 23:1-6; Luke 1:68-79; Colossians 1:11-20; Luke 23:33-43

Theme Ideas

There is a bittersweet beauty to Christ the King Sunday. The messiah foretold in Jeremiah 23, and celebrated in Zechariah's song in Luke 1, will now reign, as we read in Luke 23, from a cross on a hill. But this kingdom's first subject, a repentant thief, proclaims Jesus as king nonetheless, revealing that Christ's kingdom is not of this world. Paul's letter to the Colossians shows that early Christians found refuge and belonging in this "kingdom of the beloved Son" (Colossians 1:13). We're reminded that when every earthly kingdom falls short, we still belong to Christ, the king of self-giving love.

Invitation and Gathering

Centering Words (Luke 23)

> May God's thoughts become our thoughts. May Jesus' way become our way. And may the Spirit be our guide until love reigns throughout the earth.

Call to Worship (Jer 23, Luke 1, Luke 23)

> Prepare the way of the Lord.
> Make your hearts ready for the coming king.
> > **We will be merciful to prepare our hearts**
> > **for the king of mercy.**
> > **We will seek justice to prepare our world**
> > **for the king of peace.**
> Prepare the way of the Lord—
> the one who has given the ultimate gift of love.
> > **We will offer our very best as we help**
> > **build God's kingdom of justice and joy!**

Opening Prayer (Luke 23, Jer 23)

> Christ our king, reign in our hearts
> > and grant this world your peace.
> We rest from our busy pursuits
> > and our ceaseless motion
> > > to seek the kingdom you will bring.
> In our songs of praise, in our prayers,
> > and through ancient words of scripture,
> > > restore our souls to peace.
> Reign in our hearts,
> > that your love may change this world,
> > > for it is the only power that can do so,
> > > > through the grace of Christ, our Lord.
> Amen.

Proclamation and Response

Prayer of Confession (Luke 23)

Jesus, remember us when you come into your kingdom.
We exalt you as king
   because you did not stoop to the level
      of those who mocked you,
         even as you suffered on a cross.
When they taunted and tempted you to fight back,
   you overcame their hate with love.
Forgive the times when we succumb
   to our meaner instincts.
Teach us to answer acts of hate
   with greater expressions of love.
Forgive us and free us from our fears, dear Christ,
   until your grace reigns in our hearts
      and throughout the world. Amen.

Words of Assurance (Luke 23)

"Truly I tell you, today you will be with me
   in Paradise," says the Lord.
In the name of Jesus Christ, you are forgiven.
Amen.

Response to the Word (Matt 6)

Inspire us, dear Christ, to love every neighbor,
whether friend or foe.
   **May your kingdom come on earth
   as it is in heaven.**
May your church be a powerful force for good.
   **May your will be done on earth
   as it is in heaven.**
Help us feed every neighbor who is hungry
and who feels abandoned.

Give us this day our daily bread.
Cast out all evil, injustice and oppression.
Forgive our trespasses, and deliver us from evil.
Jesus, remember us when you come into your kingdom
May your kingdom come on earth
as it is in heaven. Amen!

Offering Prayer (Jer 23, Luke 23, Luke 1)
God of Grace, we offer you these gifts
in gratitude for your greater gifts
of grace and peace.
May our offerings plant seeds of hope and good news
for all who long to see your kingdom
and yearn to taste the goodness of your love.
In your holy name, we pray. Amen.

Sending Forth

Benediction (Luke 1, Luke 23)
Let us depart, changed by God's grace,
and filled with God's Spirit.
Let us go to share the love of Jesus,
the king of peace. Amen.

Hymn Suggestion
"Jesus, Remember Me"

November 28, 2019

Bill Hoppe

Color

Red

Scripture Readings

Deuteronomy 26:1-11; Psalm 100; Philippians 4:4-9; John 6:25-35

Theme Ideas

God is gracious, selfless, giving, faithful, steadfast, constant, generous, nurturing, and loving. The Lord is all of these things and so much more. How can we comprehend a power so immense and indescribable that it can bring an entire universe into being with a single command? How can we comprehend this same power at work in our individual lives, giving us the assurance that we are loved and cared for? We can only respond as God's people and offer our unending and undying thanksgiving.

Invitation and Gathering

Centering Words (John 6)

Have we come here this day seeking blessings for ourselves, or have we come seeking the creator and the giver of all good things?

Call to Worship (Ps 100, Phil 4)

Rejoice in the Lord always!

Again, I say rejoice!

Our Lord is good, and we are God's people!

God's steadfast love is eternal!

We will enter the gates of the Lord

with praise and thanksgiving!

Give thanks to the Lord!

Bless God's holy name!

Rejoice in the Lord always!

Again, I say rejoice!

Opening Prayer (Deut 26, Ps 100, John 6)

Gracious Lord, creator of all, giver of life,

we praise you!

We worship you in humility and gratitude.

Surrounded by your love and care—

we live and breathe,

we laugh and cry,

we labor and rest.

When our souls faint within us,

you satisfy our hunger with the bread of life,

and satisfy our thirst with living water.

With joy and thanksgiving,

we celebrate the unselfish bounty

you have bestowed upon us! Amen!

Proclamation and Response

Prayer of Confession (Deut 26, Ps 100, Phil 4, John 6)

Lord, your selfless generosity
  provides all that the world needs,
    yet we often keep your gifts for ourselves.
Forgive us when we are thankless and indifferent
  to the needs of others.
Rather than open our mouths in praise or song,
  we keep silent.
We forget how deeply you care for us,
  and we're blind to the abundance
    that surrounds us.
Restore us, renew us,
  and fill our hearts again with your love.
Show us what it means to be truly grateful,
  and return us to your presence. Amen.

Words of Assurance (Deut 26, Ps 100, Phil 4)

In times of famine and plenty, the Lord is constant.
God sustains us and gives us the things we need.
Our prayers and pleadings are heard.
The Lord is near: God is present with us.
The indescribable peace of the Spirit enfolds us.
All that is good, true, pure, noble, gracious,
  lovable, and praiseworthy—
    this is what God has done for us.
Thanks be to God.

Response to the Word (Deut 26, John 6)

With arms opened wide and signs of wonders,
  you have brought us to your side—
    a place filled with more
      than we could ever want or need.

We find ourselves in a land
    flowing with milk and honey.
How can we not believe all you have told us?
How can we not trust all you have shown us?
We will follow the one you sent to guide us,
    the bread of life come down from heaven,
        the one who gives life to the world.
Lord, give us this bread always.
In your name, we pray. Amen.

Thanksgiving and Communion

Offering Prayer (Deut 26, Ps 100)

Lord, we were born with nothing
    but the breath you breathed into us.
All that we have become,
    all that we have created,
        and all that we have worked for;
    all this was made possible through you.
We return what you have given to us
    as an offering of our thankfulness,
        and as a celebration of your love.
Gracious Creator, to you we offer our worship
    and our praise! Amen!

Sending Forth

Benediction (Ps 100, Phil 4)

Beloved, know that the Lord is God.
It is the Lord who made us.
We are God's people.
All that is true, all that is wonderful,

all that is just and pure,
all that is good and beautiful and right—
all of this is a magnificent and indescribable gift.
Think about these things!
Keep doing the things you have learned and received,
the things you have heard and seen,
and the God of peace will be with you!
Amen and amen!

December 1, 2019

First Sunday of Advent, Year A Begins

B. J. Beu
[Copyright © B. J. Beu. Used by permission.]

Color

Purple

Scripture Readings

Isaiah 2:1-5; Psalm 122; Romans 13:11-14; Matthew 24:36-44

Theme Ideas

Today marks the beginning of Advent—the time of waiting for the salvation of our God. Isaiah and the psalmist proclaim the day when all people will come to Jerusalem and worship the Lord. This will be a time of peace—a time when nations will beat their swords into plowshares and their spears into pruning hooks (Isaiah 2:4). The epistle and Gospel readings speak of our need to be vigilant as we wait for the Lord's return. Salvation is nearer to us than when we first began to believe, so be vigilant. The Lord will come as a thief in the night and catch many unaware. In this time of joyful preparation, let us prepare our hearts anew to receive the author of our salvation.

Invitation and Gathering

Centering Words (Rom 13)

The time has come to wake from sleep, for salvation is nearer to us now than when we first came to believe.

Call to Worship (Isa 2)

People of the living God,
come to the mountain of God.
   Prepare the way of the Lord.
Sisters and brothers in Christ,
prepare your hearts to hear the word of God.
   Prepare the way of the Lord.
Children of the Holy Spirit,
walk in the light of God.
   Prepare the way of the Lord.
Come! Let us worship.

—Or—

Call to Worship (Matt 24)

Keep awake.
   Christ is coming.
Wait for the Lord.
   Love is coming.
Prepare the way.
   Hope is coming.
Worship the Lord.
   Christ is coming soon.

Opening Prayer (Isa 2)

God of power and might,
   your majesty is greater than the highest mountain,
      your glory more radiant than the summer sun.

As the days grow dark and the sun's light wanes,
  warm our hearts with the radiance of your love,
    that we might find our courage
     and walk by the light of the moon.
As nations rise up against nation,
  strengthen our desire for peace in your name,
    that we might beat our swords into plowshares
     and our spears into pruning hooks. Amen.

Proclamation and Response

Prayer of Confession or Prayer of Yearning (Rom 13)
Eternal God, your offer of salvation
  is a gift beyond price.
We know that the night is far gone
  and that the day is near,
    but we struggle to rouse ourselves from sleep.
We long to open our eyes
  and behold the glory of your dawn,
    but our eyelids have grown heavy
     and the light stings our eyes.
We yearn to heed your summons
  and make a great pilgrimage of faith,
    but our need for rest seems greater.
Call us once again, Holy One,
  for we long to hear your voice
    and know that salvation is near. Amen.

Assurance of Pardon (Ps 122, Rom 13)
Hear the good news: Salvation is nearer to us now
  than when we first came to believe.
The one who came as child long ago,
  will awaken our hearts and give us peace.
Thanks be to God.

Passing the Peace of Christ (Isa 2, Rom 13)
Open the eyes of your hearts and witness the glory of our salvation as nations are called once more to beat their swords into ploughshares. Let us express our joy and gratitude as we share signs of the Prince of Peace.

Response to the Word (Rom 13)
The time has come to wake from sleep.
Salvation is nearer to us now
than when we first came to believe.
The night is far gone.
The day is near.
Lay aside the works of darkness.
We will walk in the light.
The time has come to wake from sleep.
Salvation is nearer to us now
than when we first came to believe.

Thanksgiving and Communion

Offering Prayer (Rom 13, Matt 24)
We may not know the day or time of your coming,
but we know that it is time to wake from sleep
and to put on the armor of light.
In gratefulness for calling us as your own,
we offer you our thanks and praise.
Receive the gifts of our hands,
and use them to bring light to the darkness
and hope to places of despair,
through your Son, the Prince of Peace.

Sending Forth

Benediction (Isa 2, Rom 13)
Go forth in faith during this season of Advent
and put on the armor of Christ's light.
> **As the days grow short and the sun's light wanes,**
> **we will shine for all the world to see.**
Go forth in love during this time of waiting
and embrace the peace that passes all understanding.
> **As disciples of the Prince of Peace,**
> **we will beat our swords into ploughshares**
> **and our spears into pruning hooks.**
Go with God.

December 8, 2019

Hans Holznagel

Color

Purple

Scripture Readings

Isaiah 11:1-10; Psalm 72:1-7, 18-19; Romans 15:4-13; Matthew 3:1-12

Theme Ideas

Signs of hope and peace come from many places. They may be seen in a government that sets things right for the poor, meek, and needy; in a prophet of wisdom, understanding, and equity; and in a people who know the power of repentance, who live in harmony with one another, and who seek knowledge of the reconciling world that God envisions.

Invitation and Gathering

Centering Words (Isa 11, Ps 72)

Signs of Advent hope and peace abound. Let us catch God's vision for our world.

Call to Worship (Isa 11, Ps 72, Rom 15)

May your earth yield prosperity for everyone, O God.
May the poor be defended,
the oppressed delivered.
May enemies live in peace.
May no one hurt or destroy.
May all the world rejoice.
May we be agents of your joy and peace,
for this is your mighty vision for our world.
May timid hearts turn bold.
May we believe it can be so.

Opening Prayer (Matt 3)

Visionary God,
in this season of preparation and reflection,
let us see, as through your eyes,
the way the world can be.
Hope, peace, joy, and love
are more than just nice things that *could* be.
Help us work to make them *really* be—
as clothing and water,
as food and fire.
Make us bearers of your promise to the world,
that all may know the power of your holy love.
Amen.

Proclamation and Response

Prayer of Confession (Isa 11, Ps 72, Rom 15)

We thank you, O God, for bearers of hope and peace
in all times and all places:
for those who govern,
when they set things right for the poor,
meek and needy;

for anointed prophets,
who speak and act in your spirit—
in wisdom, understanding, and equity.
And we thank you for reminders, gentle or urgent,
that we, too, should be agents of harmony,
reconciliation, peace, justice, and righteousness.
Make us advocates of your vision for the world. Amen.

Words of Assurance (Isa 11:9b NRSV, Rom 15)

As the prophet Isaiah proclaims,
"The earth will be full of the knowledge of the LORD
as the waters cover the sea."
This sure vision is ours.
Let us embrace God's promise. Amen.

Passing of the Peace (Rom 15:7 NRSV)

"Welcome one another," writes the apostle Paul, "just
as Christ has welcomed you, for the glory of God." In
this spirit, let us greet each other with a sign of joy and
peace.

Response to the Word (Isa 11, Matt 3)

May the Spirit of God take root in our hearts
and bear good fruit in our lives. Amen.

Thanksgiving and Communion

Offering Prayer (Isa 11, Ps 72)

May these gifts further God's vision
of a world of justice, righteousness, equity
and prosperity the world over. Amen.

—Or—

Offering Prayer (Isa 11)
> We thank you, Holy One,
>> for all your good gifts,
>>> especially the gifts of prophecy, promise,
>>>> and calls for preparation.
> As a thankful response to these gifts,
>> we offer our belief, our commitments, our money,
>> that we may hasten the time
>>> when no one will hurt or destroy
>>>> on all God's holy mountain.

(*Joanne Brown*)

Sending Forth

Benediction (Rom 15:13 NRSV)
> "May the God of hope fill you with all joy
>> and peace in believing,
>> so that you may abound in hope by the power
>> of the Holy Spirit."
> Go in Advent hope and peace.

December 15, 2019

Third Sunday of Advent

B. J. Beu

Color

Purple

Scripture Readings

Isaiah 35:1-10; Luke 1:47-55; James 5:7-10; Matthew 11:2-11

Theme Ideas

Today's Advent readings share a common theme: The promises of God are sure, even if they are not immediately at hand; Christ will surely come, but it may be awhile. Even in the face of suffering, we are called to believe that God's promises will be fulfilled. Isaiah prophesies hope and growth, even in the midst of desolation and despair. In spite of her young age and her difficult circumstances, Mary sings confidently that God lifts up the lowly and vindicates the pure of heart. James calls for patience and perseverance as we wait for the Lord. Advent is a time to remember such faith—a time to trust God's promises.

Invitation and Gathering

Centering Words (Isa 35, Jas 5)

Wait for the Lord. Strengthen your hearts, for the coming of the Lord is near.

Call to Worship (Isa 35)

Wait for the Lord: God is coming to save us.
The eyes of the blind will be opened,
and the ears of the deaf will hear once more.
Wait for the Lord: Christ is coming to heal us.
The lame will leap like a deer,
and the tongue of the mute will shout for joy.
Wait for the Lord: The Spirit is coming to renew us.
All things will be made new.
Come! Let us worship.

Opening Prayer (Luke 1, Jas 5)

As the days darken and the winter winds blow,
come to us, Promised One,
in our time of waiting.
Keep the vision of your salvation before our eyes,
where the blind receive their sight,
the lame are made to walk,
and the lowly are lifted up.
Shine the light of your healing love
into the darkness of our land,
that all may see your glory
and know that salvation is at hand.
Live in and through us during this Advent season,
that we might be messengers of your grace
and instruments of your peace. Amen.

Proclamation and Response

Prayer of Confession or Prayer of Yearning (Jas 5)
God beyond time and space,
    be with us in our time of waiting.
We long to place our trust in your promises,
    but it often seems like we are on our own.
We yearn to be found faithful in our waiting,
    but your kingdom seems so far away.
We seek the strength of your mighty hand,
    but are betrayed in our weakness.
We dream of being people of perseverance,
    but our work often seems fruitless.
Heal our doubts, O God,
    and nurture the seeds of hope in our hearts,
      that our souls may find peace
        as we wait for your arrival. Amen.

Words of Assurance (Jas 5)
Be patient, sisters and brothers,
    for the promises of God are sure.
May your hearts be at peace,
    for the coming of the Lord is near.

Passing the Peace of Christ (Matt 11)
Jesus sends us ahead to prepare for his coming. Let us prepare our hearts to receive the Prince of Peace anew by sharing the peace of Christ with one another.

Response to the Word (Luke 1)
May our souls magnify the Lord of love.
    May our spirits rejoice in God, our Savior.
For the Mighty One has looked upon us with favor.
    The Holy One has done great things for us.

From generation to generation, God's mercy is shown
to those who worship in spirit and in truth.
God's strength brings justice to the lowly.
Surely mercy and goodness will follow us
all the days of our lives.
And we will dwell in the house of Lord forever.

Thanksgiving and Communion

Offering Prayer (Luke 1, Jas 5)
Just as a farmer waits patiently for the rains
to nourish the crops of the fields,
you call us to be patient as we wait
for our gifts to bear fruit
and bless those in need.
For you fill the hungry with good things
and show mercy to your people.
As we dedicate today's offering to your use,
give us the wisdom to be faithful stewards
of your gifts;
give us the strength to be holy instruments
of your love and grace. Amen.

Sending Forth

Benediction (Matt 11)
Go and tell others what you hear and see.
The blind receive sight and the lame walk.
Go and tell others the hope we have found.
The deaf hear and the dead are raised.
Go and tell others the promise of God's kingdom.
The poor receive justice and mercy

and the weak find strength.
Go and proclaim the good news.
There is new life in Christ.

—Or—

Benediction (Luke 1)
Go forth and magnify the Lord.
We will rejoice in God, our Savior.
Go forth and live in the Lord.
**We will draw strength from the one
who scattered the proud
and brought down the powerful
from their thrones.**
Go forth and bless God's holy name.
**We will give glory and honor
to the Lord, our God.**
Go with God.

December 22, 2019

Fourth Sunday of Advent
Karen Clark Ristine

Color

Purple

Scripture Readings

Isaiah 7:10-16; Psalm 80:1-7, 17-19; Romans 1:1-7; Matthew 1:18-25

Theme Ideas

These scriptures are among the most stark Advent 4 readings in the three-year lectionary cycle. With Christmas Eve just two days away, our readings from Isaiah and the psalmist seem more like admonishments than celebrations. This is the only year when the lectionary focus is primarily on Joseph in the last Sunday before Christmas. His story of trust in the midst of uncertainty is a possible focus. Lean into the journey toward Bethlehem and the promise of God with us.

Invitation and Gathering

Centering Words

"Faith is a place of mystery, where we find the courage to believe in what we cannot see and the strength to let go of our fear of uncertainty." —*Brené Brown*

Call to Worship (Matt 1)

When an angel of the Lord appeared to Mary,
Mary said yes, even in the midst of the unknown.
When an angel of the Lord appeared to Joseph,
Joseph said yes, even in the midst of uncertainty.
When we consider the origins of our Christian faith
in the midst of mystery and glory, we say yes to God.
When we celebrate the birth of Christ,
we proclaim God is with us, Emmanuel.
Come! Let us worship.

Opening Prayer (Matt 1)

God with us, Emmanuel,
as we draw near to the manager,
focus our attention to your presence among us.
As we consider the love, care and faith
of Mary and Joseph,
strengthen our faith.
As we prepare our hearts and homes for Christmas,
be our peace. Amen.

Proclamation and Response

Prayer of Confession (Isa 7)

Loving God, Isaiah proclaimed one
who would resist evil and choose good.

We seek your grace and forgiveness
　　for those times when we have not chosen well.
We seek your compassion and mercy
　　for those times when our choices were based
　　　　on fear and mistrust,
　　　　　　rather than love and care.
We confess our weakness
　　and rejoice in the gift of grace we have
　　　　through your Son, Christ Jesus. Amen.

Words of Assurance

In the name of Jesus Christ, you are forgiven.
In the name of Jesus Christ, you are forgiven.

Response to the Word (Matt 1)

As we consider the responsibility
　　that Mary and Joseph accepted from the Lord—
　　a responsibility that changed their lives forever—
　　we ponder the requests you make of us.
Give us the courage to accept your call on our lives
　　of faith. Amen.

Thanksgiving and Communion

Offering Prayer (Isa 7, Matt 1)

In this season of giving, O God, Emmanuel,
　　receive our gifts and transform them into gifts
　　　　that help others know your presence
　　　　　　in their lives today.
May we welcome weary sojourners;
　　may we provide shelter for those in need;
　　　　and may our lives be gifts to all your children.
Amen.

Sending Forth

Benediction (Matt 1)

> Go to prepare a place in your hearts and homes
> for God your Creator, Emmanuel.
> Go to prepare a welcome for the Christ child,
> God with us, Emmanuel.
> Go to prepare an opening for the Holy Spirit,
> the breath of God among us, Emmanuel.

December 24, 2019

Christmas Eve

Mary Scifres
[Copyright © Mary Scifres. Used by permission.]

Color

White

Scripture Readings

Isaiah 9:2-7; Psalm 96; Titus 2:11-14; Luke 2:1-20

Theme Ideas

Light in the darkness, angels in the heavens, a star in the sky, the greatness of God's presence.... This is a night of glorious appearances—a night of beauty, grace, and love.

Invitation and Gathering

Centering Words (Isa 9, Luke 2)
Look to the heavens; look to the light; look to the love of God, and discover the magic of this miraculous night.

Call to Worship (Ps 96, Luke 2)
Sing a new song to God,
as we join with the songs of old.

Glory to God on the highest.
Sing with the heavenly angels,
who rejoice with us on this holy night.
Glory to God on the highest.
Sing a new song to God,
as we join with the songs of old.

Opening Prayer (Titus 2, Luke 2)
God of grace and God of glory,
shine upon us as we reflect upon
the shining light of your love.
Reveal your presence here
as we sing songs of the angelic chorus
and hear words of prophets of old.
Through your songs and stories,
remind us of your Incarnate Love,
born as a tiny child named Jesus.
In the light of your glory and grace,
we pray. Amen.

Proclamation and Response

Prayer of Confession (Isa 9, Titus 2)
God of grace and God of glory,
pour out your grace upon us.
Bring salvation to our weary world
and to our fragile lives.
Shine light in the darkened landscape
of our sins and sorrows,
that we may see your light
and receive your mercy.
In the light of your glory and grace,
we pray. Amen.

Words of Assurance (Isa 9, Titus 2)

The people walking in darkness have seen a great light.
We, who have known darkness and despair,
> upon us the light of God's mercy and grace is shining.

Grace upon grace is ours,
> never more visible than on this glorious night
> of love.

Passing the Peace of Christ (Isa 9, Titus 2)

As the Prince of Peace brings peace into the madness of our weary world, let us share the peace of Prince Jesus with signs of love and with greetings of grace.

Introduction to the Word (Isa 9, Luke 2)

A child is born to us, a son given to all the world. As we hear the familiar story this night, may we listen anew for signs of God's glory and grace.

Response to the Word or Call to Worship (Luke 2)

Sing with the angels:
Christ is born!
Shine with the stars:
Christ is born!
Rejoice in God's glory:
Christ is born!

Thanksgiving and Communion

Invitation to the Offering (Luke 2, Matt 2)

As the angels brought songs, may we bring our gifts and praise. As the shepherds brought reports of their visions, may we bring testimonies of God's vision in our lives. As the sages brought gifts, may we bring our gifts to share at the manger of Christ.

Offering Prayer (Isa 9, Titus 2)
Holy Child of Bethlehem, bless these gifts,
that they may be the grace of God
for a community in need;
that they may be the light of Christ
for people who dwell in darkness;
and that they may be the Spirit of peace
for a world at war with itself.
Bring your peace into our darkness,
and flow through our lands
with your glorious love.

Sending Forth

Benediction (Luke 2)
Return to your homes glorifying God.
Reenter your lives rejoicing in God's grace.
Go to tell the world all you have heard and seen.

December 25, 2019

Christmas Day
B. J. Beu

Color

White

Scripture Readings

Isaiah 52:7-10; Psalm 98; Hebrews 1:1-4, (5-12); John 1:1-14

Theme Ideas

Although the birth of Jesus is the focus of Christmas, themes of grace and salvation abound in today's readings. These texts remind us to sing and rejoice, not only as we celebrate Christ's birth, but throughout the year. This need is as ancient as the word of God itself. Today, of all days, is a time to convey the glory of this ancient miracle and feel its enduring power to transform our lives.

Invitation and Gathering

Centering Words (Isa 52, Ps 98)

Blessed are the feet of those who come announcing peace. Blessed are the messengers who come proclaiming the miracle of Christ's birth.

Call to Worship (John 1, Ps 98)

In the beginning was the Word,
and the Word was with God,
and the Word was God.

Make a joyful noise to the Lord, all the earth.
Let the seas roar and the mountains quake.

Everything came into being through the Word.
What came into being was life,
and the life was the light for all people.

Sing to the Lord a new song,
for God has done marvelous things.

The Word became flesh and blood,
and lived among us to bring all people to the light.

Let heaven and earth break forth into joyous song,
singing praises to our God.

The light shines in the darkness
and the darkness has not overcome it.

Christ, our light, shines forth in glory.
Christ, our life, brings grace and truth.
Let us worship. Alleluia!

Opening Prayer (Isa 52, Ps 98, John 1)

How beautiful upon the mountains, O God,
are messengers of your light and love
who come announcing peace.
How delightful in the congregation
are voices singing the good news
of our salvation.
How wonderful in the wretched places of our world
are heralds of your justice and mercy
who proclaim the coming of your reign.
Bring us your peace, Holy One,
and remind us once more

of the good news of our salvation,
    that we might sing with joy this day,
        and shout for all the world to hear.
Christ is born. Alleluia!

Proclamation and Response

Prayer of Confession (Isa 52, Heb 1)
God of new beginnings,
    when our eyes become fixed
        on the glitz of the season,
            turn our gaze once more to the hills,
                where your messengers come
                    bringing news of hope and peace;
    when our attention becomes trapped
        in bitter conflicts of the past,
            remind us once more,
                that you speak a freeing word to us
                    through your Son.
Free us from the surface trappings of this day,
    and refocus our hearts on the glory of Christ's birth,
        that we may be messengers of peace
            and children of your Spirit. Amen.

Words of Assurance (Ps 98, Heb 1)
With righteousness and equity,
    Christ has come to bring justice and grace,
    love and compassion.
Through the tender mercies of our God,
    and the glorious love of Jesus Christ,
    we are forgiven!

Passing the Peace of Christ (Isa 52)
> How beautiful are the feet of those who come announcing peace. How radiant are the eyes of those who shine the light of God's love. With blessings of peace and love to share, let us turn to one another and offer signs of God's blessings this Christmas day.

Thanksgiving and Communion

Invitation to the Offering (Isa 52)
> In a cynical world that puts personal well-being ahead of the common good, let us remind the skeptics of the beauty of messengers who come proclaiming peace. Let us show the doubters that we, the people of God, truly do believe what we profess. Let us share the gifts we have received from God, that others might know that Christ is alive in our hearts, and is born anew in us each day as we share Christ's love with one another.

Offering Prayer (Heb 1, John 1)
> God of light and love,
>> receive our gifts this day,
>>> and strengthen our commitment
>>>> to share the love we feel at Christmas
>>>>> with those in need throughout the year.
> Send these offerings into the world
>> on the wings of your angels,
>>> that those who are touched by our gifts
>>>> may feel the healing warmth
>>>>> of your holy fire.
> Shine in our lives and in our ministries,
>> that the whole world may see
>>> your joyous light. Amen.

Sending Forth

Benediction (Isa 52, Ps 98, John 1)
Make a joyful noise to the Lord.
We will sing praises to our God.
Walk in the light of Christ.
We will share the joy of God's holy love.
Be messengers of hope and peace.
We will proclaim the good news.
Christ is born. Alleluia!

December 29, 2019

First Sunday after Christmas

B. J. Beu

Color

White

Scripture Readings

Isaiah 63:7-9; Psalm 148; Hebrews 2:10-18; Matthew 2:13-23

Theme Ideas

The saving love of God unifies these readings. Isaiah proclaims that it was no angel that saved the people of old, but the very presence of God. The psalmist proclaims that all creation praises God: heaven and earth, young and old, birds of the air, and every creeping thing. How can we keep from singing God's praises? Hebrews depicts the suffering of Christ for our salvation, and Matthew recounts Herod trying to rid himself of a potential rival by slaughtering the innocent. Salvation should be treasured and celebrated all the more for the cost it entails on the innocent.

Invitation and Gathering

Centering Words (Isa 63)

It is no messenger or angel that saves us but God's very presence. Praise the Lord.

Call to Worship (Ps 148)

Praise the Lord from the highest heavens.
> **Praise God, sun and the moon;**
> **sing for joy, you shining stars.**

Praise the Lord from the deepest seas.
> **Praise God, fire and hail;**
> **dance in ecstasy, snow and frost.**

Praise the Lord from the hearts of the faithful.
> **Praise God, young and old;**
> **laugh with mirth, wise and meek.**

Worship the Lord our God.
> **Pay homage to the ruler of heaven and earth.**

Opening Prayer (Isa 63, Heb 2, Matt 2)

God of holy mystery,
> it was no heavenly stranger
> > that came to save us;
> it was no happy accident
> > that freed us from captivity;
> it was no careless gesture
> > that showed us the ways
> > > of life and death.

You are our light and our salvation.
You alone are worthy of our worship and praise.
In this season of Christmas,
> remind us once more of what you offer:
> > a love born of endless searching,

a connection born of deep longing,
a future born of selfless sacrifice.
Be with us now,
for we are your people
and you are our God. Amen.

Proclamation and Response

Prayer of Confession or Prayer of Yearning (Matt 2)
Merciful God, we long to be more
than we have become.
In this season of joy,
remove the scales from our eyes,
that we might respond with passion and purpose
to the needs all around us.
We rejoice with the angels
who proclaimed Christ's birth
and warned Mary and Joseph
to flee from Herod's soldiers,
but we give little notice to the tyrants
who cause the death of innocent children
in our world today.
We celebrate the star in the heavens
that guided the wise men from the East
to the Christ child,
but we ignore the light shining within us
that might help us find our way
when all other lights go out.
Open our eyes and our hearts this day,
that we might be new creations,
transformed and reborn in the love
and the joy of Christmas. Amen.

Assurance of Pardon (Isa 63, Ps 148)
> It is no messenger or angel who saves us—
>> it is the very presence of God.
> God is the horn of our salvation.
> In Christ, God's salvation dwells with us
>> and makes us whole.

Passing the Peace
> Before Jesus could bring God's peace here on earth, his family had to flee to Egypt to escape Herod's soldiers. Before we can be instruments of Christ's peace, we too must escape the forces of death and destruction that seek to imprison us. Let us offer one another strength and encouragement as we pass the peace of Christ.

Introduction to the Word (Isa 63:7)
> Let us recount the gracious deeds of God and the praiseworthy acts of the Lord. Let us meditate on everything the Holy One has done for us in God's steadfast mercy.

Response to the Word (Heb 2)
> Praise the Lord from the highest heavens.
> Praise the Lord from the deepest seas.
> Let the sun and the moon,
> and all the shining stars, praise God.
> Praise the Lord, O people of God.
> We praise the author of our salvation.

—Or—

Response to the Word (Ps 148)
> Praise God from the highest heavens.
> **Praise God from the deepest seas.**
> Praise God in the wind and the rain.

Praise God in the snow and the frost.
Praise God with love in our hearts.
Praise God with joy in our souls.
Let all creation praise God.
Praise God!

Thanksgiving and Communion

Offering Prayer (Isa 63, Ps 65, Heb 2, Matt 2)
God of glory, we thank you for your many blessings.
You plant fruit trees to feed your creatures,
    and cause the sun and moon
        to provide warmth and light.
Your steadfast love provides everything we need
    to walk in faithfulness,
        even amidst the trials and tribulations of life.
In thankfulness and praise for the love that guides us
    and the hand that fills our lives with good things,
        we dedicate this offering
            as signs of our love and service.
In the name of Christ,
    the pioneer of our salvation,
        all praise and glory be unto you. Amen.

Sending Forth

Benediction (Isa 63, Matt 2)
As we journey through the Christmas season,
    more than a star guides us.
As we traverse the hillsides of faith,
    more than a messenger shows us the way.
As we ride the rapids of our lives,

more than an angel shields us from harm.
When we live the truth of Christmas,
more than the delight of holiday meals blesses us.
In Christmas, we taste the joy of our salvation.
We touch the presence of the living God.
Go with God.

Contributors

Laura Jaquith Bartlett is an ordained minister of music and worship, who serves in The United Methodist Church's Oregon-Idaho Annual Conference. She is the immediate past president of the Fellowship of United Methodists in Music and Worship Arts (FUMMWA), and was the Worship and Music Director for The UMC's 2016 General Conference.

B. J. Beu is a spiritual director and life coach who pastored churches in the United Church of Christ for more than twenty years. B. J. lives in Laguna Beach, California, with his wife, Mary, and their son, Michael, when he is not at California State University Northridge studying film.

Mary Petrina Boyd is pastor of Langley United Methodist Church on Whidbey Island. She spends alternating summers working as an archaeologist in Jordan.

Mary Sue Brookshire is a United Church of Christ pastor in San Diego, California, which comes as a surprise to her on many levels.

Joanne Carlson Brown is a United Methodist minister serving Tibbetts UMC in West Seattle, Washington. She lives with her *anam cara*, Christie, and Thistle, the Wonder Westie.

James Dollins is senior pastor of Anaheim UMC in Southern California, where he lives with his wife, Serena, and sons, Forrest and Silas. He is a lover of music, intercultural ministries, and God's creation

Karen Ellis is a United Methodist pastor who lives with her husband and children in Tustin, California. She enjoys writing liturgy for worship and children's stories.

Rebecca J. Kruger Gaudino, a United Church of Christ minister in Portland, Oregon, teaches biblical studies and theology at the University of Portland, and also writes for the Church.

Hans Holznagel has worked as a newspaper reporter, chief operating officer of a theater, and on the staff of the national ministries of the United Church of Christ in such areas as communications, mission education, administration and fundraising. He currently serves as development and marketing manager at Cogswell Hall in Cleveland, Ohio, a residence for low-income adults with disabling conditions. He and his wife, Kathy Harlow, live on Cleveland's Near West Side, where they belong to Archwood UCC.

Karen Clark Ristine is a journalist turned United Methodist minister, an editor, writer, preacher and fan girl of the Holy Spirit.

Mary Scifres is a United Methodist pastor, motivational speaker, teacher, and author who brings both inspiration and expertise for twenty-first century leadership in creative worship, church growth, change management, visioning, and strategic planning. Learn more at www.maryscifres.com.

Deborah Sokolove is Professor of Art and Worship at Wesley Theological Seminary where she also serves as the Director of the Henry Luce III Center for the Arts and Religion.

NOTE: The special entries for Watch Night/New Year (Joanne Carlson Brown), Ascension Day (Ciona Rouse), Thanksgiving Day (Bill Hoppe), and Christmas Day (B. J. Beu) are reprinted from earlier editions of the *Abingdon Worship Annual*.

Indexes

Scripture Index

Communion Liturgies Index

Password for online access at abingdonpress.com:
Galatians3:28

As of spring 2018, you also now have the option of subscribing to the *Abingdon Worship Annual* digital edition to allow easy access at any time when developing worship services. Go to www.ministrymatters.com and click on the "Subscribe Now" drop-down menu at the top left of the website. Select "Worship Annual" and follow the prompt to set up or login to an account. The print version or the digital version or both in combination are available for subscription to the *Abingdon Worship Annual*. Subscriptions renew each year until you choose to stop. Since we seldom know where you purchased the print or eBook edition of the annual, unless you purchased a print or online subscription at MinistryMatters.com, we are unable at this time to grant subscriber access to the online digital edition at ministry matters.com.

2019 Lectionary Calendar

Lectionary readings in the *Abingdon Worship Annual 2019* relate to Lectionary Year C (January 6–November 24) and Lectionary Year A (December 1–29). Bolded dates below correspond to Sundays and other liturgical events in the calendar year.

2019

JANUARY 2019						
S	M	T	W	T	F	S
	1	2	3	4	5	
6	7	8	9	10	11	12
13	14	15	16	17	18	19
20	21	22	23	24	25	26
27	28	29	30	31		

FEBRUARY 2019						
S	M	T	W	T	F	S
					1	2
3	4	5	6	7	8	9
10	11	12	13	14	15	16
17	18	19	20	21	22	23
24	25	26	27	28		

MARCH 2019						
S	M	T	W	T	F	S
					1	2
3	4	5	**6**	7	8	9
10	11	12	13	14	15	16
17	18	19	20	21	22	23
24	25	26	27	28	29	30
31						

APRIL 2019						
S	M	T	W	T	F	S
	1	2	3	4	5	6
7	8	9	10	11	12	13
14	15	16	17	**18**	**19**	20
21	22	23	24	25	26	27
28	29	30				

MAY 2019						
S	M	T	W	T	F	S
			1	2	3	4
5	6	7	8	9	10	11
12	13	14	15	16	17	18
19	20	21	22	23	24	25
26	27	28	29	30	31	

JUNE 2019						
S	M	T	W	T	F	S
						1
2	3	4	5	6	7	8
9	10	11	12	13	14	15
16	17	18	19	20	21	22
23	24	25	26	27	28	29
30						

JULY 2019						
S	M	T	W	T	F	S
	1	2	3	4	5	6
7	8	9	10	11	12	13
14	15	16	17	18	19	20
21	22	23	24	25	26	27
28	29	30	31			

AUGUST 2019						
S	M	T	W	T	F	S
				1	2	3
4	5	6	7	8	9	10
11	12	13	14	15	16	17
18	19	20	21	22	23	24
25	26	27	28	29	30	31

SEPTEMBER 2019						
S	M	T	W	T	F	S
1	2	3	4	5	6	7
8	9	10	11	12	13	14
15	16	17	18	19	20	21
22	23	24	25	26	27	28
29	30					

OCTOBER 2019						
S	M	T	W	T	F	S
		1	2	3	4	5
6	7	8	9	10	11	12
13	14	15	16	17	18	19
20	21	22	23	24	25	26
27	28	29	30	31		

NOVEMBER 2019						
S	M	T	W	T	F	S
					1	2
3	4	5	6	7	8	9
10	11	12	13	14	15	16
17	18	19	20	21	22	23
24	25	26	27	**28**	29	30

DECEMBER 2019						
S	M	T	W	T	F	S
1	2	3	4	5	6	7
8	9	10	11	12	13	14
15	16	17	18	19	20	21
22	23	**24**	**25**	26	27	28
29	30	**31**				

CPSIA information can be obtained
at www.ICGtesting.com
Printed in the USA
FSHW022224140119
55032FS